SINGAPORE
A PICTORIAL HISTORY 1819–2000

First published 1999 by Archipelago Press, an imprint of
Editions Didier Millet, in association with the **National Heritage Board**.
Reprinted 2000 (twice)

EDITIONS DIDIER MILLET

64 Peck Seah Street

Heritage Court

Singapore 079325

NATIONAL HERITAGE BOARD

61 Stamford Road

#02-01 Stamford Court

Singapore 178892

Consultant Editor and Author	:	GRETCHEN LIU
Advisor	:	LILY TAN
Publisher	:	DIDIER MILLET
Editorial Director	:	TIMOTHY AUGER
Editor	:	ELAINE EE
Researchers	:	G. UMA DEVI, GENEVIEVE GASPAR, JOYCELYN SHU, SALLY OH POH WAH
Designer	:	JOSEPH G. REGANIT
Photography copyist	:	ALBERT K. S. LIM
Production Manager	:	EDMUND LAM

Colour separated by Colourscan Co. Pte Ltd

Printed by Tien Wah Press (Pte) Limited

ISBN 981–3018–81–X

PICTURES ON pp. 1–9 AND pp. 16–17

p. 1, On the Padang, Malay boys pose with Raffles statue, c. 1910; pp. 2–3, The shophouses of Boat
Quay, c. 1870; pp. 4–5 Kampong boys, 1930s; p. 7, The junction of Cross Street and South Bridge
Road, 1890s; pp. 8–9, Collyer Quay, 1930s; pp. 16–17, Chinese junks in the harbour, 1890s

SINGAPORE
A PICTORIAL HISTORY 1819–2000

GRETCHEN LIU

ARCHIPELAGO
PRESS

MINISTRY OF
INFORMATION
AND THE ARTS

NATIONAL HERITAGE BOARD

CONTENTS

ACKNOWLEDGEMENTS

Many people have played a role in the creation of this book, but it is the support of the National Archives that has been essential in bringing it to completion. I am deeply indebted to Senior Director Lily Tan for her cheerful moral support and efficient assistance. Two Archives staff have been with the project from inception, and have rendered invaluable assistance along the way: Head of Reference Genevieve Gaspar and Archives Record Assistant Sally Oh Poh Wah are acknowledged with pleasure and gratitude. Assistant Director G. Uma Devi and Joycelyn Shu became involved at different stages, and their enthusiasm is much appreciated.

The Ministry of Information and the Arts (MITA) has been unstinting in its support, from initial concept to final proofs. Mention must be made of former Permanent Secretary MITA BG (Retd) Tan Chin Tiong who initiated the project, and the following officers: Dr Ismail Sudderuddin, Director, Publicity and Programmes Division; Dr K. U. Menon, Senior Deputy Director, Research and Planning; Karen Tan Wee Chin, Deputy Director, Publicity and Programmes Division; and Mr Pitt Kuan Wah, Deputy Director, Heritage. To the MITA photographers—Supervisor Stephen Chew, Goh Lick Huat and Tan Chuan Leck—a special thank you.

The Singapore History Museum enabled images from their collection to be put on transparency for reproduction. The smooth completion of this task was assured by the Director, Museum Collections, Loh Heng Noi, Deputy Registrar Linda Cheong and Museum Assistant Tay Ji Hiong. Deputy Director Lim Guan Hock's scrutiny of the early chapters is also appreciated. Access to the Charles Dyce material at the National University of Singapore Museum was arranged by T. K. Sabapathy, Senior Lecturer, School of Architecture; and Szan Tan, Assistant Curator, South and Southeast Asian Arts Collection.

Gratitude is expressed to the individuals who generously shared their private collections and family albums. Lee Kip Lin, whose passionate interest in Singapore's physical development has long been a source of inspiration, allowed us to include his rare early Singapore photographs. Francis Lee Wai Ming shared his own 1950s photographs, as well as the prewar images taken by his father Lee Poh Yan. Others who loaned snapshots are Chia Chin Siang, Ameer Jumabhoy, Ivy Kwa, Marjorie Lau, Pat Loh and Liu Kang. In New Zealand, John Hall-Jones, graciously provided John Turnbull Thomson's drawings of Singapore in the 1840s.

The problem of assembling post-1980 images for Chapter Five was considerably eased by the generosity of photographers Albert Lim, Wendy Chan, Luca Invernizzi Tettoni and Russell Wong. Statutory boards and government organizations responded speedily to requests, and thanks go to LTC Gabriel Chan Eng Han, Head of Operations and the Publicity Branch of the Singapore Army; Dr Kenson Kwok, Director of the Asian Civilizations Museum and Public Education Officer Juniper Chua; Ms Rennie Loh, National Arts Council Arts Administrator; Ms Stella Tay Hwee Choo, Senior Clerical Officer in the HDB Library; Annie Wong of TCS; as well as the URA, Land Transport Authority and the Preservation of Monuments Board. Among the arts groups, a special thanks to Stephanie Green and the Singapore Repertory Theatre, film maker Eric Khoo, Michelle Lim of Theatreworks and Ng Siew Eng of Singapore Dance Theatre. At *The Straits Times*, Francis Ong of the Photo Desk and Koh Bee Lian from The Straits Times Library were enormously helpful. David Lim, captain of the 1998 Mount Everest expedition, was wonderful in agreeing so quickly to loan his transparencies.

Heartfelt appreciation is expressed to those who lent a helping hand along the way: in Singapore they are Tim Auger, Associate Professor Ernest Chew, Goh Eck Kheng, Richard Helfer, Maniza Jumabhoy, Mrs Kuo Shang Wei, Associate Professor Albert Lau, Peter Lee, Herbie Lim, Ronnie Lim Eng Lian, Jean Marshall, Dr John Miksic, Didier Millet, Iskander Mydin, Syed Haroon Aljunied, Jill Quah and Julie Yeo; in Japan, Eijiro Yoshioka, Curator at the Tokyo Fuji Art Museum; and in the United States: Maria Umali of the Gillman Paper Company, the staff of the Peabody Museum in Salem, Massachusetts, and Roberta Wue; in the United Kingdom, William Schupbach and Heather Ercilla of the Wellcome Institute, Lindsey Macfarlane of the National Maritime Museum, the Foreign and Commonwealth Office Library and Annabelle Teh Gallop of the Prints Department, the British Library, and to friends Dr John Bastin, Mary Clemmey, John Falconer and Yu-Chee Chong.

Production of the book was very much a team effort. The key players were photographer Albert Lim, whose patient studio work produced excellent transparencies; designer Joseph Reganit, ever amenable, patient and willing to change; and editor Elaine Ee. Calm, sensible, obliging yet firm, it would be difficult to find an editor more professional and enjoyable to work with.

Finally to Thai Ker, Daniel and Kristin, thank you for your understanding.

EYES OF THE NATION

Singapore's history is well-charted territory. The material is as rich, exciting and diverse as the island's multiracial population—from articles on ancient Singapura and archeological finds on Fort Canning, to academic and popular books exploring colonial rule. Recent years have seen the publication of books exploring the Japanese Occupation and recording in detail the road to nationhood. Then there are the commemorative books. These range from ambitiously large and impressively illustrated compendiums to small but illuminating histories of individual schools, communities and organizations. *Singapore: A Pictorial History 1819–2000* has benefited from all of this material, as well as from the historians, sociologists, politicians and journalists who have explained with passion and precision their subject.

Here, however, it is the picture that tells the story: faded pencil sketches, brilliant watercolours, engravings, lithographs and a few paintings, but mostly photographs—from the first views produced in the 19th century, to the work of late 20th century professionals. With eloquence, they tell the story of a society originally composed mainly of immigrants, and of the island they transformed from a fishing village to a great metropolis and a thriving city state.

Images were gathered from diverse sources over a two-year period. The majority are from the National Archives of Singapore and the Singapore History Museum. Both institutions have seen their photographic collections considerably enriched by recent donations and acquisitions. Museums in Europe, Japan and the United States of America yielded some unusual material. Several private collectors, both in Singapore and abroad, allowed access to rare images. Still others generously shared their family albums.

If the search for new and arresting images was a voyage of discovery, the selection and organization process required ruthless editing. The reject pile grew large indeed. The criteria for selection? Firstly, the images had to have a strong sense of place and, with few exceptions, all are of the island. Secondly, the images had to be informative as the book was conceived as essentially documentary, and the material is arranged to tell a story. Thirdly, the book presented the opportunity to showcase the best examples that could be unearthed, and high standards were maintained in regard to the quality of the originals. Finally, some images proved absolutely irresistible, somehow so compelling in their composition or content that they begged to be included.

In organizing the material a straight chronological approach has been adopted. There are five chapters, each receiving roughly equal space. The first takes the reader from 1819 to 1869, a neat half-century that saw the settlement take root and steadily grow. The second chapter starts with the opening of the Suez Canal in 1869, and ends with the colony's centenary celebrations in 1919. Chapter Three documents the years between the two world wars, a shorter period but one which saw substantial physical and social changes. Chapter Four starts with the coming of World War II to Singapore in 1941, ends with separation from Malaysia in 1965 and includes the major political events of the era. In Chapter Five, we attempt to bring the Singapore story up to date, a near impossible task given the extraordinary changes of the last 35 years, and the enormous proliferation in the taking of photographs.

The settlement's first few decades were recorded in artists' impressions and engravings. The earliest known surviving picture of the settlement is the pencil sketch drawn in 1823 by Lieutenant Philip Jackson, an army engineer and an accomplished surveyor and draughtsman. The sketch (see page 22) shows a cluster of primitive huts along a beach that could be almost anywhere in

ABOVE John Thomson's cartes de visite, 1860s. Mary Scott (right) married Cursetjee Frommurzee, a Parsi, in Singapore in 1862. After her death in 1868, their three children, Sorab and Rustom (left) and Isabella were sent to England. The photographs survived among family papers.
FACING PAGE Rarest of the rare. Palanquin and drivers, daguerreotype by Jules Itier, 1843. This is the earliest known surviving photographic portrait.

Battery Road looking from Raffles Place towards Fullerton Square, G. R. Lambert & Co., 1890s. Lambert's main photographic studio was for many years in Gresham House which was located down the road and on the right-hand side.

Southeast Asia, except for the familiar curve of Government Hill (Fort Canning). It is now in the British Library and was probably drawn especially at Raffles' request to replace the one lost when his homeward-bound ship *Fame* caught fire and sank not far from Singapore, destroying in one terrible night the magnificent bounty assembled during years of dedicated collecting.

Many of the artists who followed in Jackson's footsteps were drawn to that same view. Sketchbook in hand, they positioned themselves on boats near the shore, and recorded their impressions of the seafront. Through their eyes, we see the town develop. The buildings become more permanent, more impressive, and the skyline is soon unmistakably that of Singapore.

Some artists were visitors, recording impressions during a short interlude on their way to some distant destination. Others shaped the island even as they recorded it. John Turnbull Thomson, resident from 1841 to 1853, surveyed the island, designed buildings and was a prolific artist. His works (see pages 34–5) are carefully preserved by descendant John Hall-Jones in New Zealand. Thomson's natural curiosity drew him to subjects as diverse as stone-cutters at work on Pulau Ubin, *attap* houses along Rochor River and the muddy half-formed streets of Chinatown. All scenes are rendered with attention to detail, as if Thomson saw himself as the custodian of a small slice of the settlement's history.

The oldest known surviving photographic images of Singapore (see pages 10 and 36) date from 1843, and are the legacy of Frenchman Jules Itier. He was travelling as the head of a commercial mission to China and the East Indies, and carried with him the newly manufactured apparatus to produce daguerreotypes. Named after fellow Frenchman, Louis Daguerre, the daguerreotype—'the mirror with a memory'—was the first practical form of photography.

Daguerre, a scenic artist who had specialized in painting stage sets for the opera and popular theatres, was only one in a generation of inventors obsessed with the possibility of fixing fleeting images. But his method, announced in 1839, was initially the most significant. The technology, however, was less than perfect: it was unpredictable; each image was unique and fragile and could not be duplicated. Protection came in the form of a bulky case or glass covering. Within 20 years, the daguerreotype was obsolete, surpassed by a far superior way of fixing images. This was the wet collodion process of sensitizing and processing glass negatives—from which any number of finely detailed paper prints could be made. Announced to the world in 1851, it triggered an explosion in photography as its commercial benefits were quickly appreciated in the age that also produced the railway and the telegraph.

Some 150 years after this breakthrough, we wonder how the world ever managed without photography. Photographs have become so ingrained in our way of life that we rarely give them a second thought. They seem part of the air that we breathe. They frame our world and guide our most basic sense of reality. And they excite our sense of discovery. Fox Talbot, one of the earliest experimental pioneers of photography, was the first to comment on this, writing in *The Pencil of Nature* in the 1840s that 'it frequently happens, moreover—and this is one of the charms of photography—that the operator himself discovers on examination,

perhaps long afterwards, that he had depicted many things he had no notion of at the time. Sometimes inscriptions and dates are found upon buildings, or printed placards more irrelevant are discovered upon their walls.'

Several European photographers stopped at Singapore, saw potential for business and stayed. Among them was John Thomson, who would become one of the most celebrated photographers of the 19th century. But in the early 1860s, he was just starting out. Perhaps the attraction of Singapore lay in his brother William who ran a business in Battery Road supplying provisions to ships. Thomson was resident for only a few years, and photographs of Singapore attributable with certainty to him are exceedingly rare. The Tokyo Fuji Art Museum is one of the few repositories, and several of Thomson's images reproduced from the museum in Chapter One demonstrate his superb technical and artistic skill.

Singapore at the end of the 19th century—prosperous, less isolated and more developed—is comprehensively portrayed in Chapter Two in photographs by G. R. Lambert & Co. The firm opened in 1877, and was for several decades the largest of several firms in Singapore selling topographical views of the island. Its commercial success reflected the thriving business climate triggered by the opening of the Suez Canal in 1869. Customers browsed through the 'finest collections of landscape views in the East, comprising about 3,000 subjects relating to Siam, Singapore, Borneo, Malaya and China', and purchased the photographs as souvenirs when photography was beyond the reach of the average traveller. However, competition from less expensive, mass-produced postcards and the spread of amateur photography

In 1904, Wilson & Co. advertised themselves as a 'household name throughout Malaya'. Their studio at No. 186 Orchard Road, formerly the premises of G. R. Lambert & Co., is known to have operated from c. 1902 to c. 1918.

From c. 1910 to the mid-1920s, Lee Brothers Studio was a landmark along Hill Street. Brothers Lee Poh Yan (right) and Lee King Yan moved their business out of Chinatown (left) possibly to attract a more cosmopolitan clientele.

rendered Lambert's views obsolete by 1910. Fortunately, fine examples have survived in private albums and public collections around the world.

It is also in Chapter Two that we first see the work of true amateurs—photographers with no special technical or scientific experience. The invention at the end of the 19th century of small cameras, improved lenses, the dry plate and rapid printing paper increased photographic output considerably. The hand camera—forerunner of today's 35-millimetre cameras—also increased the scope of photography, for with it many subjects considered beyond photographic limits were brought within grasp. Spontaneous, intimate and rooted in real situations, these images record everyday life and are a pleasing contrast to the more formal professional views.

By the 1920s, more Chinese were becoming active amateurs. Their lively, personal and unusual images enormously enrich Chapter Three. Through their eyes we see a different aspect of the city, less polished and perfect than postcard views. Among the works that have survived are those of schoolteacher Lim Lam Soon. He set up a darkroom in his Joo Chiat home, developed his own prints and mounted them in albums, each photograph carefully captioned and dated. His son, Lim Eng Lian, thoughtfully donated them to the Singapore History Museum. Another amateur photographer is the elusive Mr Goh whose stunning photograph of Holloway Lane appears on the jacket. Several of his prewar albums were donated to the National Archives of Singapore. Yet about him little is known.

Another genre of photography featured in the early chapters is studio portraiture. At the end of the 19th century, European firms like G. R. Lambert & Co. catered to the upper end of the market

Malay procession, 1930s. From the albums of photographs donated to the National Archives of Singapore by the Goh family.

while the masses were served by numerous Chinese firms whose names survive on the elaborate cardboard mounts and deckle-edged folders. The Chinese were initially slow to respond to photography. John Thomson recorded that in Singapore he employed Indians to act as his printers and assistants because 'the Chinese … at that time, refused to lend themselves to such devilry as taking likenesses of objects without the touch of human hands'. However, after moving to Hong Kong in the late 1860s, he observed that the Chinese had dropped their reservations and become ardent practitioners.

The largest known surviving collection of studio portraits is from Lee Brothers Studio. Lee Poh Yan and Lee King Yan—

Amateur efforts. Lim Lam Soon's photograph of Stamford Road (left) was taken from St Andrew's School in 1918. Wong Kwan's portrait of his desk (right) is undated.

(Left) Dr Chia Boon Leong recorded the wedding of Mr Tay Wee Soon to Miss Chia Gay Lian at Grasslands on 24 January 1927. (Right) The young Chu Sui Miong posing with a Japanese soldier.

Cantonese brothers from a large family of photographers—were master technicians who produced prints of great beauty. The brothers collaborated from around 1910 until the mid-1920s, parting amicably when large families necessitated larger incomes and, thus, independent studios. Lee Poh Yan closed his studio on the eve of World War II, but sons Lee Hin Ming and Francis Lee saved the boxes of extra or rejected prints. In 1995, Lee Hin Ming donated over 2,500 prints to the National Archives of Singapore, of which a selection is found in Chapters Two and Three.

During the 1930s, a new form of photography was gaining acceptance: photojournalism. New picture-taking possibilities opened up with the introduction of miniature cameras fitted with high speed lenses and loaded with fast film. Although the technique of the photojournalist did not differ from that of any other cameraman, the special demands made on his skill, daring and ingenuity in getting unusual pictures, and the need to turn out a print with all possible speed, made his work a special branch. The work of these intrepid cameramen features prominently in Chapter Four, which covers World War II and the political events of the 1950s and 1960s. Here we also see the work of a great variety of practitioners: ranging from professionals, like Sarawak-based K. F. Wong and the anonymous but talented photographers of the old Singapore P. R. and Information Service; and amateur enthusiasts such as Dr Carl Gibson-Hill, former director of the Raffles Museum (now the Singapore History Museum), and the enigmatic Wong Kwan, a poorly educated welder who immigrated to Singapore in 1937 with his father, never married, and left behind an astonishing collection of around 400 photographs.

Night scene, possibly Dr Carl Gibson-Hill, early 1950s. Dr Gibson-Hill was one of a diverse and enthusiastic group of photographers active in the 1950s.

Singapore in the 1960s. K. F. Wong's woman in Chinatown (left), 1962; and (right) the Bee Chun Heng Sweetmeat Shop in Victoria Street, 1963.

It is only in the final pages of the book—Singapore post-1965—that colour makes its appearance. Chapter Five draws upon the work of numerous professionals who work with 35-millimetre cameras to bring the story up to date. Here, we see the island through the eyes of both Singaporean and foreign talents. Their contemporary images, ranging from the documentary to the artistic and picturesque, illuminate and mirror our fascinating times. The veritable explosion in photography, however, made the selection process much more complex and difficult.

From around 1980, Singaporean publishers have moved into illustrated books and have produced a plethora of illustrated guides, coffee-table books and several megaprojects. *Salute to Singapore*, published in 1984 to celebrate 25 years of self-rule, brought together over 40 of the world's leading photographers, and involved 4,480 roles of film and 140,000 transparencies; similarly *Singapore: Island, City, State*, published in 1990 to celebrate a quarter century of nationhood, assembled the best of Asian and Singaporean talent. In addition, the increasing awareness of the importance of preserving the nation's heritage has resulted in the diligent documenting of the present and recent past by government bodies, from whose archives much excellent material has also been culled.

The quest for the new and the fascinating has unearthed fresh images reproduced here for the first time alongside classics without which no visual history of Singapore would be complete. What makes them so extraordinary are their unique ties to Singapore—ties to ordinary people and everyday affairs as much as to major events and personalities. From this sumptuous treasure trove, Singapore's history is vividly brought to life.

314-Chinese Junks Harbour

CHAPTER 1

IMMIGRANT SETTLEMENT
1819–1869

There were no artists present to record the moment, and the widespread use of photography was several decades away. Instead, we must use our imagination to visualize the beginning of the history of modern Singapore in January 1819: the anchoring of the East India Company ships off the jungle covered shore; the departure from the ships of company agent and Lieutenant Governor of Bencoolen Sir Stamford Raffles and his entourage in small boats; the boats navigating the entrance of a swampy river, and their occupants setting up camp on its north bank; and the meeting between the determined intruders and the shrewd local chieftain, Temenggong Abdul Rahman, who allowed them to set up a trading factory on a strip of land. We must also conjecture the demeanour of the Temenggong, the view of his village on the river and, just beyond, the crumbling ramparts of an ancient civilization on the hill called Bukit Larangan, or Forbidden Hill, as well as the appearance of the island's approximately 150 other inhabitants: the *orang laut* communities clustered along the coast and the small group of Chinese gambier farmers inland.

Raffles' objectives were free trade and the extension of British influence in the East. His mission was to establish a British trading factory in the Malacca Straits, which would complement British settlements in Penang and Bencoolen, to safeguard the route to China and to compete with the Dutch possessions of Batavia and Malacca. Singapore offered a superb location, an excellent natural harbour and an adequate supply of drinking water. The island's mythic past was an added attraction. It was hinted at in the ancient legends which Raffles, a Malay scholar fascinated by the romance of faded civilizations, knew well. Fortunately, in the Temenggong and the newly installed Sultan Hussein he found sympathetic figures who appreciated the new horizons opened up by his arrival.

We shall never know whether Raffles, who had often commissioned artists to record topographical views, monuments and natural history during his years in Southeast Asia, later considered it a terrible oversight that he had neglected to record the landscape at the time of the signing of this first treaty. But the earliest known surviving drawing of Singapore is amongst his papers. The pencil sketch by garrison engineer Lieutenant Philip Jackson (see pages 22–3) shows the tiny settlement as it was four years later, during

Raffles' third and final visit between October 1822 and June 1823. An inscription on the drawing suggests that it is similar to one in Raffles' possession which was destroyed when the ship *Fame* caught fire and sank on 2 February 1823. Six days after this disaster, Raffles wrote to his sister, Mary Ann Flint, in Singapore, asking her to entreat Jackson to send more sketches of the place 'as the former ones are gone'. Raffles finally departed from Singapore in mid-1823 with Jackson's new sketch carefully packed in his heavy trunks, amongst the new treasures he had accumulated to replace those lost in the burning *Fame*, and undoubtedly with the confidence that the humble village it portrayed would become the prosperous and 'Emporium of the East' he so ardently envisaged.

The settlement had attracted an amazing number of immigrants. By 1824, there were more than 10,000 inhabitants, and, six years later, the number had increased to nearly 17,000, with the Chinese constituting 40 per cent of the population and dominating the urban areas. Two years before Raffles' death in 1826, the last in the series of treaties was signed which secured the settlement's future. The treaties ceded the island to the British, resolved tensions with the Dutch, and combined Singapore, Malacca and Penang to form the Straits Settlements, the fourth presidency of India.

One of Raffles' most enduring legacies is the Town Plan drafted under his close supervision in 1822. Visionary and comprehensive,

ABOVE *John Turnbull Thomson's view of the airy bungalows along Beach Road in the early 1840s. Raffles Institution is on the far left.*
FACING PAGE *A view of Kampong Bugis shows houses similar to those Raffles saw upon his arrival.*

LEFT *Raffles spent little time in the city which forever expresses his fame: 10 days, from 28 January to 7 February 1819; four weeks, from 31 May to 28 June 1819; and another eight months, from 10 October 1822 to 9 June 1823.*

RIGHT *Col. William Farquhar, the first British Resident, fell out with Raffles but was extremely popular among the early immigrants. Munshi Abdullah described him as 'a man of good parts, slow at fault-finding, treating rich and poor alike and very patient in listening to the complaints of any person who went to him.' The second Resident, John Crawfurd, was a frugal Scotsman with a gruff demeanour which hid his better qualities. He guided the settlement from 1823 to 1826.*

it soon gave rise to the tidy streets portrayed on the following pages. The cornerstone of the plan was the division of the town into separate districts, each with its own function. The seat of government was allocated land on the north bank of the Singapore River, the commercial district land along the south bank. Although wealthy Asian and European merchants were encouraged to trade side by side, and could live according to their means wherever they liked, the majority of the population was settled into segregated communities. Europeans were directed to the area adjacent to the government district. Indians were given a small area around what is today Chulia Street. The Chinese, whom Raffles rightly anticipated would form the largest group of immigrants, were located south of the River, beyond the commercial area in what was to become Chinatown. The Temenggong was removed from the River to a large area between Tanjong Pagar and Telok Blangah. Sultan Hussein, whose royal status in Singapore was recognized by Raffles, settled in Kampong Glam where Arabs, Bugis and other Muslims were encouraged to establish themselves.

At a more detailed level, the plan called for a network of roads and streets of specified widths laid out at right angles, for uniform plots of land to be divided and sold and for a linear arrangement of commercial buildings and linked shophouses of specified widths and uniform facades not exceeding three storeys. An arcade-like covered passageway—the five-foot way—was introduced for the sake of regularity, conformity and weather protection.

Buildings were to be constructed of brick, with tiled roofs and solid foundations. The civic-minded Raffles included provisions for a botanical garden and religious and educational buildings.

Even as the Sultan built his palace, merchants constructed godowns along the River and real estate speculators lined the streets of Chinatown with narrow and deep shophouses showing southern Chinese influence in the roof forms and gable walls. At the same time, the jungle beyond the town was being savagely cleared by agricultural entrepreneurs. Nutmeg, in particular, was the rage, although gambier and pepper were popular as well. Amongst the first Europeans to open nutmeg plantations in the 1830s was Dr Thomas Oxley, who purchased 70 hectares of jungle from the East India Company to form the Oxley Estate. By the time the nutmeg trees succumbed to a blight in the 1840s, nutmeg estates were to be found all over the island. Beyond the nutmeg, Chinese planters cleared huge tracts of land for gambier and pepper. Gambier leaves had to be boiled soon after picking, which meant that large areas of forest were needed for the supply of wood. The unoccupied jungles were ideal for this until the soil became exhausted and all the trees cut down. The planters then moved on to Johor.

The changing face of the island during its first half-century was recorded by numerous artists, some of whom visited the settlement for a short time, such as naval surgeon and water-colourist Edward Cree (see pages 24–5), and others who lived in it for years and came to know it well, such as the merchant Charles Dyce (see pages 30–3) and surveyor–architect John Turnbull Thomson (see pages 34–5). Images of newly discovered and

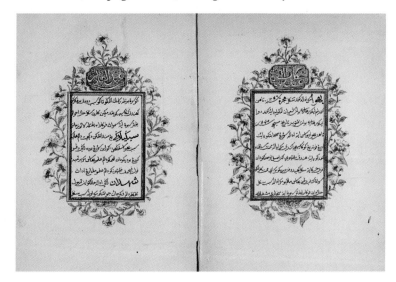

Frontispiece in Jawi script of the first edition of the Hikayat Abdullah *by Munshi Abdullah. Published in 1849, it is the earliest and most vivid account of early Singapore by an Asian. As a young boy, Abdullah had been a Malay writer for Raffles in Malacca, and in his later years he taught at Raffles Institution.*

developing places were rare and deeply appreciated: 'In describing people and countries hitherto unknown, no description given by the pen will equal one correct drawing,' observed Frank S. Marryat in the preface to his book *Borneo and the Indian Archipelago.*

Some views reached a wider audience through the medium of engraving. Advances in printing had, by the early 19th century, greatly aided the reproduction of prints in books and folios. Most of the early engravings were produced in travel books or in the reports of scientific and exploratory expeditions which stopped at Singapore, already a natural transit point on the East–West trade route. The French, in particular, were attracted to the rapid rise of Singapore as a trading centre and its strategic position in the Far East. So much so that reports from several French voyages included important engravings of the settlement during its first few decades.

As a busy port and a crossroads of travel, Singapore was an attractive location for a European photographer. By the 1860s there were several who, in addition to doing a brisk business in studio portraits, offered views of Singapore for sale. It is these remarkable images, so carefully framed and exquisitely detailed, which compose the majority of the material selected for this chapter.

The photographs show a settlement that still hardly extended more than a kilometre-and-a-half from the beach, even though the population had doubled from 35,389 in 1840 to 81,734 in 1860. The increased density was felt especially in the ethnic quarters, but even the main European residential area around Beach Road and the Esplanade was becoming more crowded and less desirable. A large part of the population was floating and transitory, and women were extremely scarce. The relative neatness of the town was frequently noted by writers, including John Cameron who observed in *Our Tropical Possessions in Malayan India*, that the 'town … [is] remarkably compact, the country may be said to come right up to its walls. There are none of those intermediate half-formed streets with straggling houses here and there, which so often disfigure the outskirts of the town. Where the town ends, the country commences; indeed it would be difficult for a piece of ground to remain long deserted for nature would soon crowd it with her works, if man did not with his.'

This was the Singapore that greeted a young and talented photographer who arrived from Scotland in 1862. Singapore was the first stop for John Thomson (1837–1921) (not to be confused with John Turnbull Thomson, surveyor–architect), who became one of the most celebrated of 19th-century photographers, his fame resting on his photographic documentation of China and the Far

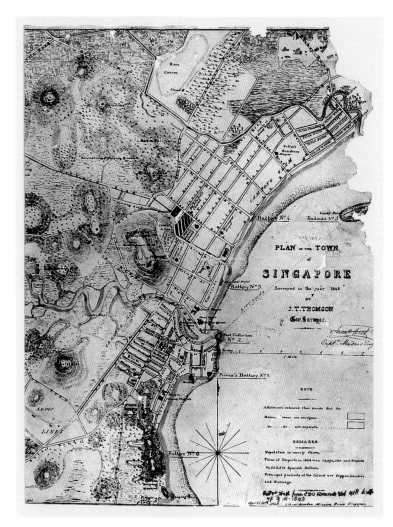

This map by John Turnbull Thomson records the development of the settlement during the 1840s.

East in the 1860s and early 1870s. Thomson was equipped not only with superb technical and artistic skills, but with knowledge of the latest advances in commercial photography in Europe. In his memoirs, *The Straits of Malacca, Indo-China and China*, Thomson recorded his first impression of Singapore, 'When I first saw it in 1861, I was startled by the appearance of the European town and since that time it has been yearly registering its substantial progress in steadily increasing rows of splendid docks, in bridges, in warehouses and in government edifices …'

Thomson had moved to Hong Kong when Singapore became a Crown Colony in 1867, and was establishing himself as a society photographer in London at the end of the 19th century as the landscape which he had so vividly recorded in Singapore was being dramatically affected by the benefits of the opening of the Suez Canal on East–West trade and the growing importance of the port of Singapore. Thomson, and the work of his contemporaries, portray that brief moment in time when the small settlement was at the end of an era and on the brink of dramatic change.

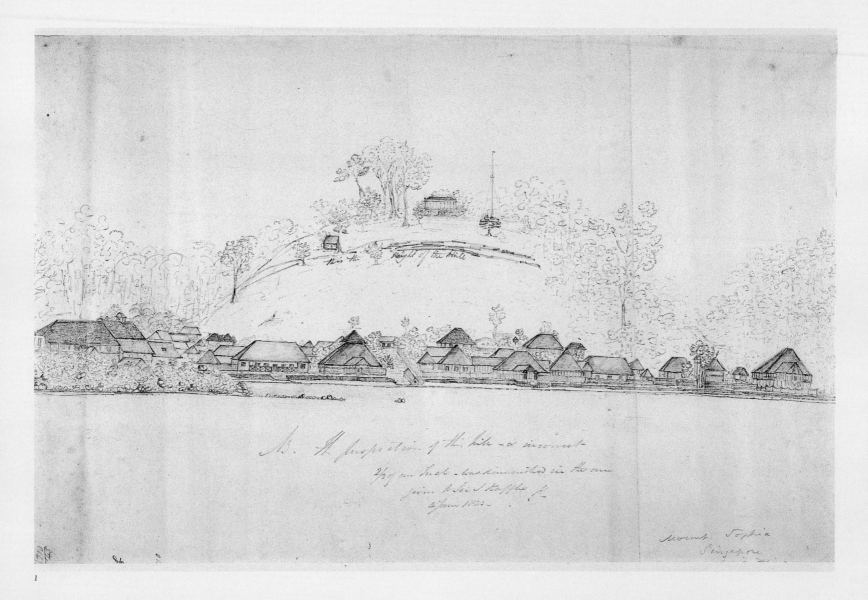

1

The earliest known drawing of Singapore is a sketch by Lieutenant Philip Jackson (1), which shows the infant town four years after its founding. Dominating the scene is Government Hill and the bungalow upon it that was built for Raffles in early 1823. The north bank of the River, the proposed Cantonment Plain, is crowded with primitive wooden and *attap* houses. These structures were later cleared.

Lieutenant Jackson, an accomplished surveyor and draughtsman, arrived in 1822 and spent the next five years as Executive Officer and Surveyor of Public Lands. His map (4) illustrates Raffles' Town Plan of 1822–3, which established guidelines for urban growth. Many of its elements remain in Coleman's map of 1836 (8) and in the city even today.

Within a few short years, regular streets of brick houses with red-tiled roofs replaced the original wooden structures in the urban area. When the unknown artists of (2) and (6) recorded their views of the sea, the plain had been cleared. By the 1850s, when other artists skilfully recorded the Singapore River (7) and a view from the sea (3), the 'Mayfair of Singapore' presented an

impressive townscape, from the turrets of government offices and the Dalhousie Obelisk, to the houses facing the open plain.

The Singapore Institution was founded at a meeting convened by Raffles on 1 April 1823. The earliest known drawing (5) shows the two-storeyed construction finished to the design of the Superintendent of Public Works, G. D. Coleman, in late 1837, when it was first used as a school. The artist, J. A. Marsh, was probably on Coleman's staff.

---

1 *View of Singapore from the sea, Lt Philip Jackson, pencil sketch, 1823*
2 *From Government Bungalow, ink and watercolour, 14 November 1828*
3 *Inscribed 'Governor's Hill, Singapore', ink and sepia, early 1850s*
4 *Plan of the town of Singapore, Lt Philip Jackson, from John Crawfurd's* Journal of an Embassy from the Governor General of India to the Courts of Siam and Cochin China, *Henry Colburn, London, June 1828*
5 *The Singapore Institution, J. A. Marsh, pen, ink and watercolour, 1841*
6 *Singapore from the sea, undated pencil sketch*
7 *Singapore River, pencil sketch*
8 *Map of the town and environs of Singapore from a survey, G. D Coleman, published 1836*

2

Singapore from the Gov.ʳ Bungalow Nov 14ᵗʰ 1828.

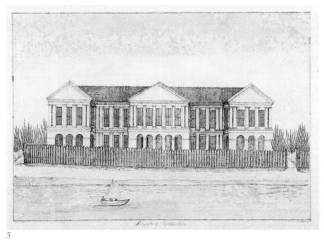

5

3

6

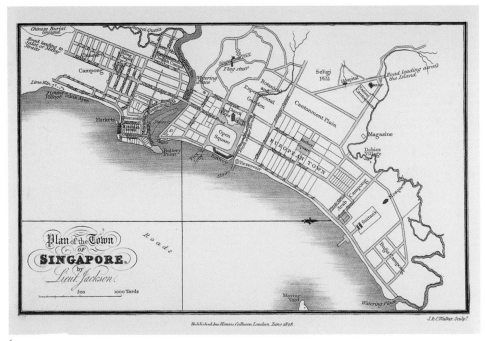

4

Plan of the Town
of
SINGAPORE
by
Lieut. Jackson.

500   1000 Yards

7

8

MAP OF THE
TOWN AND ENVIRONS
OF
SINGAPORE.
from an Actual Survey
by
G.D. COLEMAN.

Scale of One Mile

1

2

3

At Singapore June 1844

6

In the days before photography, officials of the East India Company often acquired drawing skills in the course of their training as engineer officers or draughtsmen.

Little is known of Mr Edgell, whose views (1 and 2), though somewhat distorted, strongly convey the atmosphere of those early days and of the tiny human settlement encroaching on the hilly, thickly wooded island.

The career of Edward Hodges Cree (1814–1901) has been well documented. An Englishman of Scottish extraction, Cree studied medicine at Dublin and Edinburgh before serving as a surgeon in the Royal Navy for 30 years, 10 of which (1840–50) were in the Far East. From his first day on board ship, Cree kept a journal which he illustrated with watercolours, and which was preserved by his family.

Cree first visited Singapore for a fortnight in 1840. During a later visit, in 1844, he was entertained in the homes of some of the settlement's most famous pioneers: the Portuguese Dr Jose d'Almeida (4) and wealthy Chinese merchant Hoo Ah Kay, popularly known as Whampoa (5).

Dr Jose d'Almeida came to Singapore in 1825, set up a dispensary, and later built up a business dealing in Chinese goods. He was also one of the pacemakers of Singapore society. Of d'Almeida's large family of 10 daughters and four sons Cree recorded, 'They are all very musical and get up delightful concerts in their house, twice a week, to which some of us have a general invitation. The ladies are not good looking—Portuguese seldom are … but they sing and play various instruments divinely … It was a lovely moonlight night and the large room open to the verandah all round made it cool, so we were able to enjoy the quadrilles and waltzes and a little flirtation.'

Cree's view of the waterfront (3) depicts with accuracy the mouth of the river, Maxwell's House, the Residency on Government Hill and the bungalows designed by G. D. Coleman facing the Esplanade.

4

Mr Whampoa's Entertainment Sep 21 1844

5

1 *View of Singapore from the sea*, H. E. Edgell, watercolour, 1820s
2 *View from Government Hill*, H. E. Edgell, watercolour, 1820s
3 *Singapore from the sea*, Edward Cree, watercolour, 1844
4 Inscribed '*Signor Jose d'Almeida's musical party, 26 Sept. 1844*', Edward Cree, watercolour
5 Inscribed '*Mr. Whampoa's Entertainment, 21 Sept. 1844*', Edward Cree, watercolour
6 *Street sellers, Singapore*, Edward Cree, watercolour, 1844

1

2

1 Inscribed 'View of the Town and Roads of Singapore from the
  Government Hill, c. 1822–4', engraved by John Clark, London, 1830

2 View from Government Hill of the Plain, Singapore River and
  Chinatown, c. 1822–5, uncoloured lithograph, artist, engraver and
  publication date unknown

3 View from Government Hill of Singapore River and Chinatown,
  c. 1824, engraved by Langlume, coloured lithograph, Paris, 1828

4 Inscribed 'Vue du Temple Protestant à Sincapour, 1837', engraved by
  Louis Bichebois, coloured lithograph, Paris and London, 1845–52

5 Inscribed 'View of Government Hill, the English Burial Ground,
  and the Armenian Church', engraved by G. S. Madeley, lithograph,
  London, 1840

6 Inscribed 'Environs de Sincapour, 1837', engraved by Jean Louis
  Tirpenne, coloured lithograph, Paris and London, 1845–52

3

4

5

6

The main source of early Singapore engravings are travel books and the reports of scientific and exploratory expeditions which stopped at Singapore, a natural transit point on the East–West sea route. The French, in particular, were attracted to the rapid rise of Singapore as a trading centre and its strategic position in the Far East. Several French voyages produced outstanding prints of the settlement (3, 4 and 6). These views are an important record of the blossoming of the port during its first two decades. By the end of its first decade, Singapore had largely fulfilled Raffles' commercial ambitions. Its fame as a port where traders could do their business in peace, with no burdensome restrictions or charges, had spread throughout the region.

Many of the communities in Singapore began to build permanent religious buildings. The first, and finest, Christian edifice was the Armenian Church which is depicted with some distortion in (5). Designed by G. D. Coleman, and completed in 1836, it was described in *The Straits Times* as 'one of the most ornate and best finished pieces of architecture that this gentleman can boast of'. As the Armenian Church neared completion, Coleman began work on the first St Andrew's Church, seen on the right-hand side of the view of the Esplanade (4) which is inscribed 'Vue du Temple Protestant à Sincapour'. It was completed in 1835, with a steeple added some years later. After being struck by lightning several times, the building was pronounced unsafe, and work on a new church commenced in 1861.

A form of transportation on the island was the palanquin, an enclosed horse-drawn carriage. The view of the countryside (6) shows a palanquin drawn by four horses and led by runners, or syce, with torches. Horses were scarce and expensive. The first horses imported to Singapore from Sydney in 1844 sold extremely well. The 11 animals fetched a price of $211. Horse auctions were held in Commercial Square up until the 1890s.

In 1830, the French corvette *La Favourite* visited Singapore during a voyage around the world. The ship's official artist, Edmond François Paris, made sketches of the Singapore River, which formed the basis for the pair of engravings (1 and 2).

The two engravings contain many interesting details of the buildings first constructed along the River. The European merchants built warehouses on the originally marshy south bank after it was reclaimed in 1822. South Boat Quay (2) was faced with masonry, and provided with a double row of steps for access at high and low tides. Jackson's, or Presentment, Bridge (1) was the first structure to span the River, thus giving rise to North and South Bridge Road.

The third view of the River is from the mid-1840s. On the north bank are the Landing Shed Office and, behind it, the roof of the Master Attendant's Office. Government House and the flagstaff are clearly visible on the hill, and the scene is enlivened by a variety of native craft, which also caught the eye of another artist resident in Singapore for some time, Charles Dyce. The delightful rendering of native crafts (4) is a page from his album *Sketches in the Straits* (see pages 30–3).

1 *View of Singapore River, Presentment Bridge and Government Hill, 1830, engraved by Sigismond Himely, aquatint, Paris, 1835*
2 *View from the mouth of the Singapore River, 1830, engraved by Sigismond Himely, aquatint, Paris, 1835*
3 *The Singapore River with Thomson's bridge, c. 1849–53, engraved by Vincent Brooks, coloured lithograph*
4 *Malay boats, Charles Dyce, pen and watercolour, from* Sketches in the Straits, *1847*

Malay Sampan, or Tambang

Bugis Proa.
from the Celebes

Cochin-Chinese
Tope.

Malay Trading Proa

Deep sea Fishing Boat

Malay Fishing Boat

Chinese Sampan

1

2   3

One of the most remarkable records of early Singapore is the series of watercolours and ink-and-sepia drawings by Charles Andrew Dyce in the volume *Sketches in the Straits* (3), which was dedicated to the directors of the East India Company (2).

The superb view of the River (4) takes as its vantage point the bridge connecting North and South Bridge Roads and shows the simple, utilitarian godowns of the European traders near the river mouth. Beyond are the masts of clipper ships anchored to discharge or take on cargo. The foreground is filled with bustling human activity.

The view of 'Singapore from the Roadstead' (1) illustrates just how strongly Government Hill dominated the view of the town from the sea. The settlement appears as a village nestled between it and the sea.

About Dyce little is known. He flits elusively through the pages of C. B. Buckley's *An Anecdotal History of Singapore*, always as a passing reference, never at centre stage. He was an amateur organist at St Andrew's Church and 'eventually married one of the young ladies who sang'. He designed the steeple for the Cathedral of the Good Shepherd, was Secretary of the Racecourse and a freemason. He is also listed amongst those who attended the meetings which established Tan Tock Seng Hospital and a library in the Singapore Institution. Often participating in amateur theatricals, he painted the scenery. His drop scene, a view of Singapore, was used for many years.

1 Inscribed 'Singapore from the Roadstead', Charles Dyce, ink and sepia,
  c. 1847
2 Dedication page of original album and manuscript, Charles Dyce, 1847
3 Title page of the same
4 Inscribed 'The River from Monkey Bridge', Charles Dyce, ink and sepia,
  c. 1847

4

1

2

3

4

5

6

7

'The Town and Roadstead' (1) is one of the most valuable drawings in the Dyce folio (see pages 30–1), as it depicts with great perspective, skill and clarity the buildings along the Singapore River. According to Dyce, the large building, whose roof is seen in the centre of the drawing was the public (Assembly) rooms. The unusual view of the town (2) is from the tip of Tanjong Rhu, then known as Sandy Point, along the eastern coast of the island. It shows the series of small hills which were then such a distinct characteristic of the landscape. On the left of the vista of Telok Ayer Bay (3) is the rocky base of Mount Wallich. In the distance are Telok Ayer Market and the buildings facing Commercial Square and backing onto the sea, with private jetties for loading and unloading goods.

The upper reaches of the Singapore River are featured in two watercolours. The view of Government Hill (4) shows buildings at the beginning of River Valley Road, the flagstaff and the house which was erected by Sir Stamford Raffles in January 1823 and subsequently purchased by the government. The old bridge (5) is Presentment Bridge which was built in 1822 and replaced in 1846. It is flanked by two godowns which survived well into the 20th century, that of Edward Boustead on the left and that of Yeo Kim Swee on the right.

---

1 Inscribed 'Singapore the Town and Roadstead', sepia wash, c. 1847
2 Inscribed 'Singapore from Sandy Point [Tanjong Rhu]', sepia wash, c. 1847
3 Inscribed 'The Town from the Parsi Club House', sepia wash, c. 1847
4 Inscribed 'Government Hill Singapore 1844 from the new harbour road'
5 Inscribed 'The old Bridge, Singapore, 1842, Since removed'
6 Inscribed 'New Harbour from the proposed Dry Docks', watercolour, c. 1847
7 The Esplanade, sepia wash, c. 1847

1

2

3

In 1841, John Turnbull Thomson (1821–84) was appointed Government Surveyor. He was only 21 years old, but had already made his mark surveying large estates in Penang and other parts of Malaya.

For the next 12 years, until his retirement in 1853, he served as both surveyor and engineer to Singapore, producing maps of the town, the island and the Singapore Straits. He also constructed a number of roads, bridges and buildings, including the Horsburgh Lighthouse on the exposed Pedra Branca Rock at the eastern entrance to the Singapore Straits some 54 kilometres away.

The buildings he designed included the Chinese and Seamen's Hospitals at Pearl's Hill, the Ellenborough buildings, a tower and spire for the first St Andrew's Church and the Dalhousie Obelisk which still stands (it was built in the 1850s in honour of the visit of the Governor General of India).

Thomson was also a self-trained artist. His sketches and paintings of early Singapore, preserved by his family in New Zealand, form an important visual record of the settlement.

Singapore's population in 1841 was no more than 35,000, of which only 200 were European. In his memoirs, *Glimpses into Life in Malayan Lands*, Thomson described the European part of the town as 'studded with handsome mansions and villas of the merchants and officials', while 'the Chinese part of the town was compactly built upon and resounded with busy traffic'. The Malays, he recorded, 'lived in villages in the suburbs and their houses were constructed of wood and thatched with leaves. In the Chinese and Malay quarters, fires frequently broke out, spreading devastation into hundreds of families.'

Thomson's two views of Chinatown (5 and 7) document the inland progression of shophouses from the coast. The wooden footbridge joining North and South Bridge Roads, built by Thomson (4), was widened in 1846 to take carriages, remaining in use until 1862. The imposing building to the right of the bridge is Boustead's building. Erected in 1832, it was demolished in 1925 when the road was widened. Thomson's view from Mount Palmer (6) encompasses Telok Ayer Bay and the area beyond the commercial centre of town.

4

1 *John Turnbull Thomson, undated photograph*
2 *The artist sketching, detail from painting, 1849*
3 *Inscribed 'View in Singapore Town. 1846. Hindoo Pagoda.*
  Kling Mosque', watercolour
4 *Thomson's bridge and South Bridge Road, 1840s*
5 *Inscribed 'Singapore Town from Government Hill looking South', 1846*
6 *Inscribed 'Singapore Town from Mount Palmer', 1847*
7 *View of Chinatown from Pearl's Hill, 1847*

5

6

7

1

The earliest surviving photographic views of the settlement were taken in 1844 by Jules Itier of the French Customs Service, who was travelling through Singapore as head of a commercial mission to China and the East Indies. The four quarter-plate daguerreotypes (8.3 x 10.5 centimetres) include a view of the Singapore River from Government Hill (1).

Developed by Itier's fellow countryman, Louis Daguerre, and announced to the world in 1839, the daguerreotype—'the mirror with a memory'—was the first practical form of photography. It basically involved a copper plate, with a layer of silver on one side, which was carefully cleaned and polished, and made light sensitive by contact with iodine vapours. After exposure, the latent image was developed in fumes of heated mercury, causing tiny mercury gobules to be deposited on the plate, thus giving its distinct, fragile mirror-like impression of light. After fixing, the daguerreotype was usually mounted in a leather frame, its delicate surface protected by glass. Each image was unique, and could not be replicated.

Sachtler & Co.'s views of Singapore (1–4, following pages) were taken 20 years later, and illustrate the enormous advances in photography that were made in the intervening years, as do the early morning view of Katong (2), a rare interior view (3)

and the view of the Plain and the River (4). A key date is 1851, the year of the announcement of a new British process, Scott Archer's wet collodion process, which revolutionized photography by using glass-plate negatives to produce finely detailed paper prints. Not only did this make all earlier processes obsolete, but its negative–positive process permitted unlimited printing from the original negative. The commercial benefits were obvious, triggering off an explosion in the recording of the topography of Singapore. From the early 1860s until 1874, Sachtler & Co. operated a studio in High Street where they offered Singapore views for sale.

1 *Singapore River, Jules Itier, daguerreotype, 1844*
2 *Inscribed 'Coconut Plantation Singapore—Early Morning', John Thomson, c. 1864*
3 *Inscribed (in German), 'Our living room in Singapore', Frederick George Schmidt, c. 1860*
4 *Part of Sachtler's 10-part panorama, taken from the spire of St Andrew's Church, 1863*

FOLLOWING PAGES

1 *Singapore River from Fort Canning, Sachtler & Co., 1863*
2 *Upper reaches of the River, Sachtler & Co., 1863*
3 *The Racecourse at Farrer Park, Sachtler & Co., 1863*
4 *Malay village near New Harbour, Sachtler & Co., 1860s*

2

3

4

1

2

3

4

1

2

3

4

5

Early outdoor photography was a major undertaking requiring patience and skill difficult to comprehend today. A darkroom tent had to be set up near the camera, the glass-plate negatives coated and sensitized, and the exposure time estimated based on trial and error. Problems were compounded by the humidity and uncertain chemical supplies. Yet the results were exquisitely detailed. The famous Scottish photographer John Thomson, who resided in Singapore in the early 1860s, shared his experiences in *The British Journal of Photography*, advising, 'I have generally found the early morning to be the best for photographic purposes … The temperature is lower, and for an hour or two, nature enjoys the perfect repose.'

In the view of Chinatown (1), a figure on top of Pearl's Hill gives a sense of scale to the buildings around South Bridge Road. The rooftop of Raffles Institution can be seen in the right-hand corner of the view of the European town (4). In the portrait of Europeans (5), everyone is carefully posed. Because of the long exposure time, any movement caused a blur.

1 Chinatown from Pearl's Hill, photographer unknown, early 1860s
2 Inscribed 'Convict Pier', early 1860s
3 Johnston's Pier, early 1860s
4 View of the European town from Fort Canning, early 1860s
5 Europeans at home, 1860s

1

2

By the 1860s, Singapore town was considered one of the beauty spots of the East. The person largely responsible for this was architect George D. Coleman. An Irishman from Drogheda, Coleman studied architecture in Dublin. He first visited Singapore in 1822, during which he was involved in several projects initiated by Raffles. He returned to take up residence in 1826.

For the next 15 years, he was engaged by the government to carry out revenue and topographical surveys, and to lay out and construct roads and bridges. In the 1830s, he was officially appointed Government Surveyor, and in 1833 became Superintendent of Public Works, Overseer of Convict Labour and Land Surveyor. In short, it was he who implemented Raffles' vision of an attractive, orderly and well laid-out settlement.

Coleman also maintained a flourishing private practice as an architect and contractor. He built many of the elegant houses commissioned by the Europeans and was also responsible for several places of worship as well as godowns. On the street which still bears his name, he built his own grand residence.

When he died in Singapore in 1843, he left a legacy of town development and fine public buildings which established high standards for his successors.

The unusual early view of the Esplanade (right) before any reclamation shows the Old Banyan Tree, a landmark of the time, and the neat cluster of buildings near the mouth of the Singapore River in the mid-1860s, including Fort Fullerton (2).

RIGHT *The beach, Old Banyan Tree and mouth of the River beyond, 1860s*
1 *The main means of transportation, horse and hackney carriage, 1860s*
2 *Fort Fullerton, photographer unknown, 1860s*

1

2

3

4

5

6

7

8

9

10

These pages show many of the first 'official' buildings constructed in Singapore. The oldest is the house designed by G. D. Coleman for John Argyle Maxwell (1). This refined Palladian villa of elegant proportions and detailing was for many years considered to be the island's finest building. The last major renovation, in the 1950s, converted it to the Legislative Assembly House. For this and his other buildings Coleman relied on ordinary and easily available materials: Chinese and Malaccan bricks and tiles, timber felled from the jungle, granite from surrounding islands and lime plaster from the coral reefs.

Coleman also supervised the revival of Raffles Institution (7). The original structure was poorly constructed, left unfinished and had fallen into a ruinous state. Coleman restored the ruin in 1835–7 and erected two wings, in 1839 and 1841.

Hidden behind trees (2) was the Post Office. Its inconvenient location on the north bank of the River was for many years a point of contention with merchants, whose offices were concentrated on the south bank. The first Ellenborough Market (8) was constructed by Captain C. E. Faber at New Bridge Road in 1845. The view of the Master Attendant's Office (4) shows the landward facade. The Master Attendant was the senior officer in charge of the port.

Buildings on the outskirts of town included the Colonial Jail at Outram Park (3) and the General Hospital (6) which was completed in 1860, probably at Kandang Kerbau. The location of the Central Police Station (9) is not recorded.

Construction on Empress Place (5) commenced in June 1864 and was completed in December 1867, the same year that Singapore became a British Crown Colony. It was designed as a Court House, and built by convict labourers under the supervision of engineer J. F. A. McNair. This photograph is from the Foreign and Commonwealth Office Library in London. It may have been the 'official portrait' sent home, as it was taken shortly after building work was finished, with construction dates and cost penned on the matting.

---

1 Maxwell's House, constructed 1826–7
2 Post Office, mid-1860s
3 Colonial Jail, foundation stone laid 1847, photograph, late 1860s
4 Master Attendant's Office, 1860s
5 Public offices and council chamber, 1869
6 Inscribed 'The General Hospital', c. 1869
7 Raffles Institution, first used as a school in 1836, photograph, 1860s
8 Ellenborough Market, completed in 1845, photograph, 1860s
9 Central Police Station, c. 1869
10 Iron market, probably at Clyde Terrace, under construction,
  early 1870s

By the time the photographs on this page were taken in the late 1860s, many of the 'handsome lofty mansions' in the European town had long been vacated by the merchants and government officials for less congested suburbs. Two of the three famous bungalows designed by G. D. Coleman overlooking the Padang (1 and 2) were then occupied by the Hotel de l'Europe and the third by the Masonic Lodge.

St Andrew's Church (3 and 5) was designed by Lieutenant Colonel Ronald Macpherson, Executive Engineer in 1855–7, and is one of the few surviving examples of English Gothic architecture in Singapore. The Cathedral of the Good Shepherd (4), the settlement's first permanent Catholic church, was constructed in 1843–7.

The Town Hall (6) was an architectural milestone as it marked the arrival of Victorian Classical Revivalism; its design reflected the British mid-century fascination with Italian Renaissance architecture. Designed by John Bennet and built in 1856–62, it was described in an 1892 *Guide to Singapore* as being of 'high architectural pretensions' and 'a highly ornamental building of composite architecture'.

Government House (7) was the brainchild of General Sir Harry St George Ord, the first Governor of colonial Singapore. Ord's proposal for an official residence was unpopular, the impression being that a building of such size and expense was an unnecessary extravagance. The building was designed by Colonel J. F. A. McNair who is in the right-hand corner of the photograph. In his book *Prisoners Their Own Wardens* he records, 'The whole of the brickwork, exterior plastering, and most of the flooring and interior work were effected by convict labour.'

1 *Courthouse and bungalow designed by G. D. Coleman, photograph, 1860s*
2 *Bungalows by G. D. Coleman and spire of St Andrew's Church, photograph, 1860s*
3 *St Andrew's Church, consecrated 1862*
4 *Cathedral of the Good Shepherd, constructed 1843–7*
5 *Interior of St Andrew's Church, 1860s*
6 *Town Hall shortly after completion in 1862*
7 *Inscribed 'Government House, Singapore, built by Major McNair (Grandpa) Colonial Engineer. Convict labour was used almost entirely.', 1868–9*

1

2

3

4

5

6

7

1

2

This rare photograph (right) of G. D. Coleman's Telok Ayer Market was probably taken around 1870. The market was a prominent seafront landmark, easily recognizable in many old drawings and photographs of the settlement. Completed in 1838, it continued to be used until the new Telok Ayer Market (constructed on reclaimed land in the former Telok Ayer Bay) was certified as complete on 1 March 1894.

The building was actually a replacement for an earlier failed structure: a timber and *attap* market built over the water at the western end of Market Street that was found to be structurally defective. Some supporting timber piles required immediate replacement, while the attap roof was rejected by the authorities who insisted on tiled roofs as a fire precaution. Roof tiles were duly installed, but the structure could not support the weight, and the attap was reinstated. By 1830, the market was described as being in an 'extremely unsafe state'.

Coleman, in his capacity of Superintendent of Public Works, was called upon to design a new market. He provided a 'very commodious' octagonal structure, covering an area of 1320 square metres, formed by two concentric rings of brick piers. The drum above the main roof was formed by a trio of arches, clearly visible in the photograph, on each side of the octagon. This device allowed light and air into the market. Annie Brassey in *The Voyage of the Sunbeam*, published in 1871, described the market as 'a nice, clean, octagonal building, well supplied with vegetables and curious fruits'.

The adjacent single-storeyed tiled roof structure to the left of the market was probably the fish market which Brassey described as 'situated on a sort of open platform under a thick thatched roof, built over the sea ...'

RIGHT **Telok Ayer Market, c. 1870s**
1 **Telok Ayer Market, Charles Dyce, watercolour, 1840s**
2 **Inscribed 'Town Market', engraving**

These photographs show some of the bridges which spanned the Singapore River during the settlement's first 50 years. The panorama (top) shows the wooden pedestrian bridge which connected the north and south banks during the 1860s. It was built as a short-term solution to the nagging problem of connecting Commercial Square on the south bank with the Post Office on the north bank.

The problem of a convenient connection between Commercial Square and the north bank was permanently resolved by the construction of Cavenagh Bridge (3). A cast-iron suspension bridge by P. & W. MacLellan of Glasgow, it was installed in 1869 and named in honour of Governor Colonel William Orfeur Cavenagh, the last India-appointed Governor of Singapore.

The small wooden bridge across the stream at the junction of south Boat Quay and Circular Road (1) was rarely captured in photographs, in contrast to the frequently photographed Elgin Bridge (2), connecting North and South Bridge Roads, which was completed in 1869.

Early photographers were fond of panoramic views, and the River was a favourite subject. Panorama 1 (following pages) encompasses both north and south Boat Quay. Perhaps more interesting is the view of the upper reaches (2, following pages), from Fort Canning across to Mount Wallich, Pearl's Hill and the outskirts of Chinatown. Among the buildings identifiable along the river bank are Ellenborough Market and, at the base of Pearl's Hill, Tan Tock Seng Hospital.

TOP *Master Attendant's Office, godowns at the mouth of the River and the wooden bridge which for a brief period connected Commercial Square with the north bank, 1860s*
1 *The wooden bridge at Circular Road, 1860s*
2 *Elgin Bridge, completed 1862*
3 *Cavenagh Bridge, completed 1869*

FOLLOWING PAGES
1 *South Boat Quay and the north bank, c. 1870*
2 *The upper reaches, mid-1860s*

1

2

Singapore

1

2

1

2

Bukit Larangan, Forbidden Hill, Government Hill, Fort Canning: the small hill overlooking the Singapore River has been known by many different names. During the settlement's earliest years, it was the home of the Resident, the chief British official, the site of the first botanic gardens and, until 1865, the Christian cemetery (1). It was not until 1860 that its military and strategic role came into being.

Early visitors were often amazed at the lack of defence and fortifications in so prosperous a place as Singapore. However, by 1857 a variety of factors—increased pirate activity in the region, a growing consciousness among merchants of the power of the Chinese secret societies and an awareness that international peace could not last forever—conspired to cause concern about this state of affairs.

In 1858, Captain Collyer of the Madras Engineers produced a voluminous report recommending extensive fortifications on Government Hill, but the costs were prohibitive and the report generated a fear that turning Singapore into a great military fortress might have a disastrous effect on trade. Work thus proceeded on a reduced scale. Fort Canning, including officers' quarters (2) and seven 68-pounders installed on platforms overlooking the town and harbour, was completed in 1861.

The fort was considered a failure from the first: ships could come near enough to destroy the town without coming within range of the guns, and as a refuge in time of unrest it was useless as it had no water supply.

LEFT **View from Fort Canning of the River and roads, c. 1867**
1 Christian burial ground and Kampong Glam, c. 1865
2 Inscribed 'Officers Qtrs., Fort Canning', 1860s

1

2

3

4

In 1858, George Collyer of the Madras Engineers designed an extensive reclamation scheme for the seafront. Partly financed by the merchant community, but subsidized by the government by means of the allocation of convict labour, the Quay (1 and 2) was completed in 1864 and named after its designer. By 1866, the ensemble of new buildings, 'constructed as uniform as possible' along the Quay, was completed to the great delight of the business community. The buildings were soon acknowledged as 'one of the sights of the Far East'.

Johnston's Pier (2) was constructed in 1854–5 and named after Alexander Laurie Johnston, a merchant. Passengers alighting at Johnston's Pier made their way towards Fullerton Square (4), where a Victorian fountain was erected in 1878 in memory of pioneer Tan Kim Seng. Battery Road (3) owes its name to the fact that it was the link between Fort Fullerton (built in 1829 and demolished 1873) and Commercial Square.

1 *Collyer Quay, 1870s*
2 *Collyer Quay and Johnston's Pier from d'Almeida's Pier, 1870s*
3 *Battery Road looking towards Commercial Square, c. 1870*
4 *Fullerton Square with newly installed Tan Kim Seng fountain, late 1870s*

1

Commercial Square was officially renamed Raffles Place in 1858, but its original name remained in common usage for many more years. The change was highly appropriate as it was Raffles who had insisted on placing the business centre of the town on the south side of the River, even though the terrain was entirely unsuitable, alternating between hillock and low-lying swamp. The solution was to reconfigure the land. A levelled hillock became Commercial Square, and the earth was carried off to provide solid foundations for the godowns along south Boat Quay. By the time the photographer John Thomson arrived in Singapore in 1862, Commercial Square was the premier business address. 'There are the shops, the stores, the banking houses, and the merchants' offices', Thomson wrote in *The Straits of Malacca, Indo-China and China or Ten Years' Travels, Adventures and Residence Abroad*. 'There Europeans and Chinese pursue their various occupations. But the rows of new buildings … cast a cool shade over the less assuming, antique, green venetianed structures, erected in "the good old days".'

2

1 Corner of Battery Road and the Square, late 1860s
2 North side of the Square, 1860s
3 The Square and drinking fountain, 1870s
4 South side of Commercial Square, 1860s

3

4

1

2

One of the most striking features of Raffles' Town Plan was the allotment of separate areas within the town to the different ethnic communities. The Indians were allocated land on the south bank of the Singapore River in the area around what is now Chulia Street. An early photograph of the street (1) shows buildings of virtually uniform height and character closely packed together.

Nagore Durgha (facing page) was built between 1828 and 1830 by South Indian Muslims in memory of the visit of a holy man, Shahul Hamid of Nagore, to the sandy beach of Telok Ayer Bay. History records that the land was leased to one Kanderpillai on the condition that the building erected on it would not be made of *attap* and wood.

The elaborate tower-like *gopuram* of Sri Mariamman Temple (2) has been a landmark since around 1843. The temple was established in 1823 by Naraina Pillai, a government clerk from Penang, who came to Singapore with Raffles.

FACING PAGE **Nagore Durgha, Indian–Muslim shrine at Telok Ayer Street, c. 1865**
1 *Chulia Street, 1870s*
2 *Sri Mariamman Temple, South Bridge Road, early 1860s*

1

2

3

4

5

The first Indian convicts arrived in 1825, and were accommodated in lines built for their reception between Bras Basah and Stamford Roads (4 and 5). Although there was opposition, their presence proved a boon to the town. With labour scarce and expensive, convicts were employed in backbreaking work reclaiming swamps, building roads (1), quarrying stone (2) and erecting buildings and bridges. They excelled in brick-making, carpentry and blacksmithing. Until 1873, the settlement's Executive Engineer doubled up as Superintendent of Convicts—G. D. Coleman (see pages 42–3) was appointed the first in 1833.

The convicts were also in demand as servants. They were paid for their private and public work, and those released after a short incarceration generally saved enough to set themselves up as cattle keepers or owners of bullock carts, carriages and horses for hire. Some worked at the Racecourse which was established at Farrer Park, not far from the convict lines and close to Serangoon Road, later to become Singapore's 'Little India'.

1 Indian labourers, inscribed 'Chantier de Coolies', c. 1870
2 Stone quarry, Pulau Ubin, c. 1869
3 Inscribed 'Parade of Convicts (in Convict Jail)', c. 1869
4 View from Mount Sophia of Dhoby Ghaut and Convict Jail
5 View of the Convict Jail, early 1870s

Raffles anticipated that the Chinese would eventually form the largest single ethnic community in Singapore. Thus, the entire area south of the Singapore River beyond Boat Quay and Commercial Square was set aside as their district. Chinatown developed inland from Telok Ayer Street, which faced the beach and sea. The area was dense and crowded from its earliest days. The southern limit was defined by Mount Wallich, the vantage point of the panorama (below).

The oldest and most important temple in Singapore is Thian Hock Kheng (3), established in 1842. Wak Hai Cheng Bio (1) was established by the Teochews at Phillip Street, while Tan Si Chong Su (2) was built by the Tan clan as their ancestral temple.

1

*BELOW **Panorama of the roofs of Chinatown, Telok Ayer Bay and Collyer Quay beyond, c. 1870***
1 Wak Hai Cheng Bio at Phillip Street, 1890s
2 Tan Si Chong Su, 1870s
3 Thian Hock Kheng, 1870s

2

3

1

Two designated Malay districts evolved, each around one of the leaders who had signed the documents ceding Singapore to the British. Sultan Hussein settled in Kampong Glam, while the Temenggong's village, originally near the mouth of the River, was moved to Telok Blangah.

Sultan Mosque (3) was built in 1824–6. A brick structure with a double-tiered roof in the shape of a truncated pyramid, it survived to celebrate its centenary in 1924, at which time the trustees approved the erection of the present building.

The drawing of Kampong Rochor (5) on the banks of the Rochor River is by John Thomson. Little is known of E. Schluter who vividly captured Malay customs (2 and 4) (see pages 80–1). The entrance gate of Jamae Mosque (6) has been a prominent South Bridge Road landmark since the 1820s. The portrait of a group of Malays (1) is simply inscribed 'Singapore Inhabitants'.

1 Inscribed 'Singapore Inhabitants', 1870s
2 Malay gathering, E. Schluter, watercolour, 1858
3 Malay mosque, Kampong Glam, John Thomson, watercolour, 1846
4 Malay wedding procession, E. Schluter, watercolour, 1858
5 Inscribed 'Campong Rochor. Singapore. 1846', watercolour, John Thomson
6 Malay mosque, South Bridge Road, coloured lithograph

2

3

4

5

6

1

2

3

4

On the western fringes of the town was Tanjong Pagar (6), which in Malay means 'Cape of Stakes'. Between Tanjong Pagar and Telok Blangah further west along the coast was the reserve (7) that had been set aside for the Temenggong and his followers. The area was still village-like when this photograph was taken in the 1870s, although burgeoning port facilities at New Harbour beyond were signalling the beginnings of change.

Tanjong Pagar was only one of the many Malay settlements which dotted the coastal areas for much of the 19th century (1–5). John Cameron writing in the 1860s, in *Our Tropical Possessions*, described Singapore's coastline as 'an endless panorama, most beautiful where its wild forests are untouched, picturesque where are clustered together the leaf-built houses (4) of its native villages.'

The Bugis Kampong (2 and 3) adjoined Kampong Glam. Bugis traders were for many years one of the mainstays of Singapore's prosperity, and its major link with the islands of the archipelago further east. At their peak in the mid-1830s, as many as 200 Bugis *prahu* arrived in Singapore every September to October, coming in with the southeast monsoon, anchoring off Beach Road and laden with goods to sell.

1 *Houses on Kallang River*
2 *Boat builders, Kampong Bugis*
3 *Malay village, possibly Kampong Bugis, 1870s*
4 *Malay house, 1860s*
5 *Malay houses along the coast, 1860s*
6 *Tanjong Pagar and New Harbour, 1870s*
7 *The view towards Mount Palmer, 1870s*

5

6

7

1

Until the 1860s, nearly all trade was conducted at Boat Quay. As shipping traffic increased, congestion at the river mouth worsened. The situation was aggravated by the arrival of early steam vessels which needed coal. The coal was brought to Singapore in sailing vessels, taken ashore in lighters, stored and then taken out again in lighters when required.

Anticipating the need for better facilities, shipping companies began to build wharves at New Harbour in the late 1850s. Here, steamers found that the deep water close to shore made it easier to load and unload cargo and coal.

In October 1868, the newly formed Tanjong Pagar Dock Company opened a graving dock for ship repair together with a 300-metre wharf. The wharves proved very profitable because of their location—they were about one-and-a-half kilometres from Commercial Square. This made them readily accessible by both sea and road, which was not the case with the other wharves. With the opening of the Suez Canal in 1869, steam traffic to the Far East increased to such an extent that more ships were offered than could be repaired. In 1876, it was decided that another graving dock should be constructed. In 1879, the Albert Dock opened and the wharves were extended.

One of the most notorious ships to call at Singapore was the Confederate battle cruiser *Alabama* (2). This was during the American Civil War and the cruiser was on a mission to hurt Yankee traders. On 22 December 1863, it coaled in New Harbour, having just burned several American trading vessels near the Sunda Straits. After leaving Singapore, it burnt a British-registered boat.

2

3

---

1 Facilities of the Singapore Slipway & Engineering Co. which repaired ships above the waterline
2 The Confederate battle cruiser Alabama *coaling at New Harbour, 22 December 1863*
3 Sailing ship at New Harbour, c. 1870
4 An early undated view of New Harbour showing the construction of timber piles which support the piers
5 Undated photograph, inscribed 'Wharf Waiting Room'
6 Cargo at New Harbour, 1860s

4

5

6

The luxuriance of Singapore's jungle encouraged false hopes for a prosperous agricultural future. Nutmeg, cotton, sugar, coffee and cinnamon were all attempted, and abandoned, but in the process the jungle was savagely cleared (2).

The most notable successes were gambier and pepper. In combination the two were ideal for Chinese immigrants. Gambier waste provided an excellent fertilizer to counteract pepper (4) which exhausted the soil. Gambier leaves had to be boiled soon after picking (1), so that it was necessary to have large areas of forest to supply wood for the burners. The unoccupied jungles of Singapore proved perfect for this purpose, until the soil was exhausted and the planters moved to Johor. Wealthy Teochew merchant Seah Eu Chin (1805–83) (3) controlled many gambier plantations in Singapore and Johor.

Another important commodity was gutta-percha, a gum-like resin acquired by chopping down gutta-percha trees. Although the trees had vanished from Singapore by 1847, the resin continued to be collected in Malaya and sent to Singapore for packing (facing page) and shipment.

FACING PAGE Inscribed 'Packing gutta percha at Ross's godown', 1870s
1 Processing gambier
2 Plantation, unidentified location, Singapore, 1870s
3 'Gambier King' Seah Eu Chin
4 Pepper plants, c. 1860s

By the 1860s, two main roads led out of town: Orchard Road (1 and facing page) and River Valley Road (2). John Cameron, in *Our Tropical Possessions*, described the former as lined 'by tall bamboo hedges with thick shrubbery behind and broken here and there by the portals at the entrances of the private avenues leading from it, or occasionally by a native hut or fruit shop. Many years ago, *angsana*, wild almonds, *jambu* and Weringan trees were planted along both sides ... these have now grown up to their full proportions, closing overhead, forming a complete shade to the road and giving the appearance of a very beautiful vista extending along its entire length.'

FACING PAGE **Country road, possibly Orchard Road, c. 1870**

1 *Inscribed 'Orchard Road', c. 1870*

2 *Inscribed 'River Valley Road', c. 1870*

3 *Inscribed 'Annual inundation of our garden, Singapore', John Thomson, c. 1864*

4 *Inscribed 'Rough sketch of local celebrities Singapore races 1881. Abrams hockey—Hong Lim Chinese merchant—H. H. Maharajah of Johore', J. Taylor, pen and ink with wash*

5 *Inscribed 'Orchard Road', J. Taylor, watercolour, 1879*

6 *Inscribed 'Botanical Gardens, Singapore, April 79', J. Taylor, watercolour*

7 *Country road, J. Taylor, watercolour, c. 1879*

1

2

3

4

5

6

7

8

9

10

One observer charmingly described the early suburban landscape as 'an endless succession of little knoll-like hills, covered with nutmeg and fruit trees of all varieties, and each crowned by a white-walled bungalow.' By the 1860s, a simple, elegant style of bungalow architecture had evolved, which conformed to English traditions but made concessions to the tropical climate, as these images illustrate. The houses were generally square and compact, with high, hipped roofs that had short projecting ridges. Wall surfaces were plain and unadorned. The entrance was protected by a carriage porch above which a verandah was standard in two-storey bungalows. Drawing rooms, such as the one in The Castle (7), were on the first floor together with the bedrooms. The floors were matted, and the rooms were simply furnished.

1 Draycott, 1870s
2 Ardmore, 1860s
3 Inscribed 'Ladyhill', 1860s
4 Inscribed 'Rogie of Old', 1870s
5 Prinsep's Estate, 1860s
6 The Castle, Cavenagh Road, 1870s
7 Drawing room, The Castle, 1870s
8 Cairnhill, Charles Dyce, watercolour, 1842
9 Inscribed 'Richmond Hill and Bellevue', pencil sketch, July 1861
10 Mount Echo, from an album of watercolours by John E. Taylor, c. 1879

1

2

3

The jungle closer to town was cleared by nutmeg planters, and that further out by gambier planters. Still, surviving in-between were pockets of jungle with giant trees, enormous ferns, creepers and parasites (3). Cutting through the landscape were a handful of roads, including Bukit Timah (4) which was extended to the Johor Strait in 1845, and a complex system of small rivers (6).

There were dangers in this verdant paradise, and none was feared more than the tiger. In 1835, G. D. Coleman and a group of convicts were laying out a new road through a low swampy part of the jungle about six-and-a-half kilometres from town when they were attacked (8). Fortunately, the tiger crashed into Coleman's surveying instrument; amidst the ensuing commotion the tiger turned around and disappeared into the jungle. By the 1840s, Singapore was famous for its tigers. Organized tiger hunting (7) became a lucrative sport. Apart from a $100 reward from the government for each tiger head, the flesh could be sold at a tidy sum to Chinese medicine dealers and the skin to a collector. The menace gradually diminished, but a man was killed by a tiger on Thomson Road in 1890, and two tigers were shot on Bukit Timah Road in 1896 .

1 Inscribed 'Mission Chapel Bukit Timah 1877'
2 Gharries waiting along a country lane, c. 1870s
3 View of the jungle near granite quarry, 1870s
4 Bukit Timah village, 1860s
5 Inscribed 'Passage au Sincapour', c. 1870
6 Country stream, c. 1870s
7 Captured tiger, E. Schluter, watercolour, 1858
8 Coleman attacked by a tiger, coloured lithograph, 1840s

1

2

3

4

5

6

7

8

9

10

11

From its very beginning, Singapore attracted large numbers of immigrants. Among the Malay community were immigrants from the Riau Islands, Malacca and Sumatra, comprising Bugis, Javanese and Boyanese. Although the Malays were originally the single largest group, by 1836 they were outpaced by the Chinese. Most Malays were peacefully and industriously employed as boatmen, fishermen, woodcutters and carpenters or in similar occupations.

The identities of those who posed for these photographs are unknown. Even the name of the royal-looking moustached gentleman (5) who stands erect, attended perhaps by his son, or servant, in a more casual pose, is lost to history, as are those of the equally well-dressed seated men (7 and 8) whose demeanour and clothing suggest material success at the very least, if not status and responsibility.

There are no known surviving photographic portraits of Singaporean residents until the 1860s. Thus, for our first glimpse of Singapore inhabitants we must rely on the works of artists, such as E. Schluter from whose 1858 sketchbook come the four colourful portraits (1–4).

1

2

3

4

5

6

The Indian portraits here span several decades, ranging from the drawings of E. Schluter (1–6), which were executed around 1858, to the rare photographs of children (7, 8, 10 and 13) which are from the 1870s or even the early 1880s.

Long before Raffles' arrival, Indian influence was pervasive in Southeast Asia. Raffles brought with him to Singapore an entourage that included some 120 sepoys, lascars and several Indian assistants. Singapore's Indian population initially grew slowly. Apart from the garrison and camp followers, there were only 132 Indians in 1823 out of a population of nearly 5,000. In 1849, they comprised about 10 per cent of the population, but their proportion gradually increased, peaking in 1860 at 16 per cent, then gradually falling to between 7 and 9 per cent. The vast majority were South Indian labourers and petty traders, but there were Sikhs, Punjabis, Gujaratis and Bengalis as well. By the 1860s, there were substantial Parsi, Bengali and Tamil merchant houses.

Despite their numbers and concentration in the town, the Indian community made comparatively little impact. They had no leadership and were divided in background, language and religion. In the mid-19th century, there were Parsi, Tamil and North Indian businessmen of standing, but they were important as individuals rather than as community leaders.

7

8

9

10

11

12

13

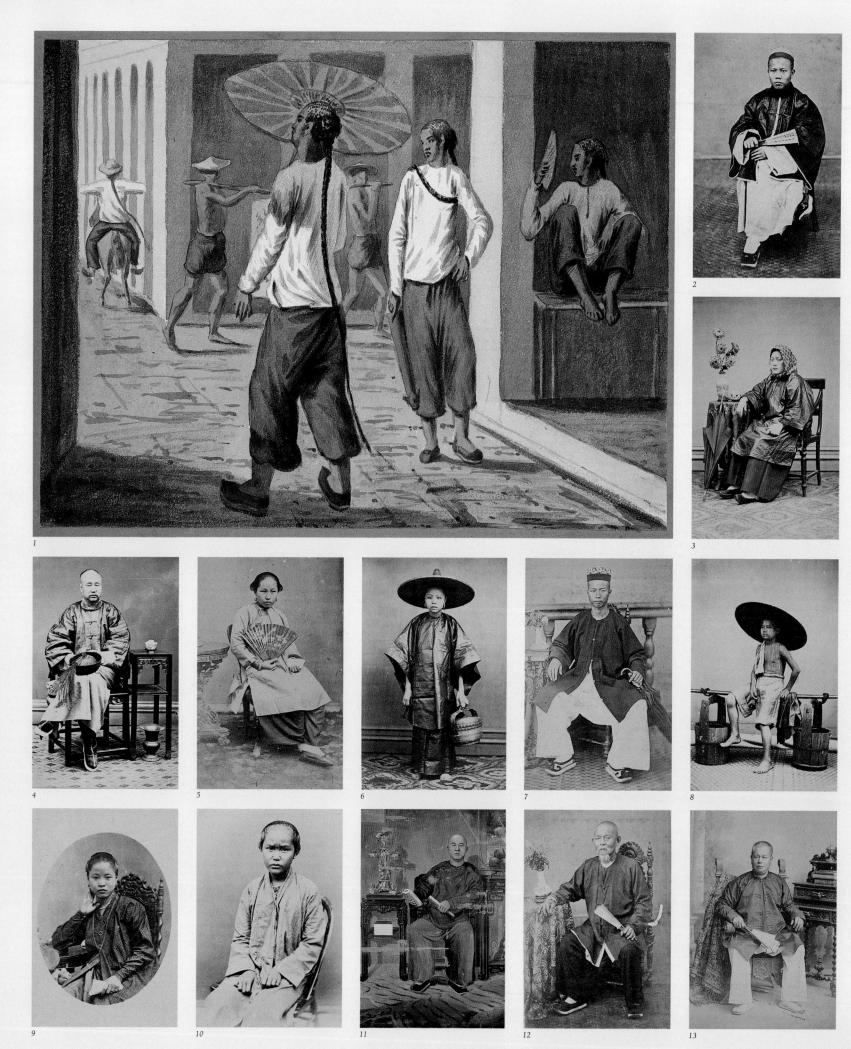

14

15

This gallery of portraits illustrates the great diversity of the Chinese community in mid-19th century Singapore. Most numerous were the Hokkiens, who, from the beginning, dominated Singapore's commercial life, followed by the Teochews. The Cantonese were generally agricultural labourers, miners or skilled artisans. Hakka immigrants usually passed through on their way to the tin mines of Malaya, but some settled in Singapore as labourers.

There was also a small group of Straits Chinese families who immigrated from Penang and Malacca. Prominent among them was Tan Beng Swee (11), the son of Tan Kim Seng. Straits Chinese men, or *baba*, wore the *baju lok chuan* consisting of a silk jacket and loose trousers (7, 12 and 13) while the women, *nonya* (9 and 10) wore *batik baju panjang* pinned with modest *kerosang* and a chequered sarong.

There was a great gulf in the standard of living between prosperous merchants and the hordes of labourers who eked out a living as itinerant vendors of wares or "travelling cookshops" (8), and as coopers, blacksmiths, tinsmiths, gunsmiths, grocers, butchers, cobblers (14), opium vendors, tailors and barbers.

Women (3, 5 and 6) were exceedingly rare. In 1864 there was only one Chinese woman to 15 men. Many female immigrants were young girls sold into prostitution. Casual photographs of children (15) are unusual and this one was taken by John Thomson, probably circa 1863 when he was resident in Singapore.

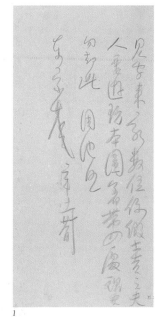

Early Singapore had its share of wealthy merchant–philanthropists and colourful pioneers. Perhaps the best known was Hoo Ah Kay (circa 1815–80) (2), also known as Whampoa, who came to Singapore in 1830. Whampoa could read and write Chinese, learned to speak English, made a fortune in business, and, in 1854, opened the first ice house. This particular venture failed, but fortune smiled on most of his enterprises, and he was reputed to be the richest Chinese merchant in Singapore. Charitable and philanthropic, he was appointed a member of the Legislative Council (5) in 1869 and an Extraordinary Member of the Executive Council. A celebrated host, he frequently welcomed guests to elaborate Western-style champagne dinners in his home on Serangoon Road, with its large and exquisite Chinese garden (facing page).

Singapore-born Cheang Hong Lim (1825–93) (6) made his money in opium and property, and actively participated in public life. In 1876, he donated funds to convert the space in front of the Police Station in Chinatown into a public garden. Hong Lim Green (7) still exists as a green space in the city.

Tan Yeok Nee (1827–1902) (3), a Teochew, rose from being a cloth peddler to a successful gambier and pepper trader, investing heavily in property. He is remembered for the Chinese mansion he built along Tank Road which is today a gazetted national monument.

FACING PAGE **Whampoa in his famous garden, 1870s**
1 *An invitation to visit Whampoa's garden*
2 *Portrait of Whampoa*
3 *Portrait of Tan Yeok Nee*
4 *German engraving of Whampoa's gate from* **Das Buch für Alle**
5 *Members of the Legislative Council, including Whampoa (standing, second from right), posing with Governor Harry St George Ord at Government House, 1873*
6 *Cheang Hong Lim (seated, second from right) and family*
7 *Hong Lim Green*

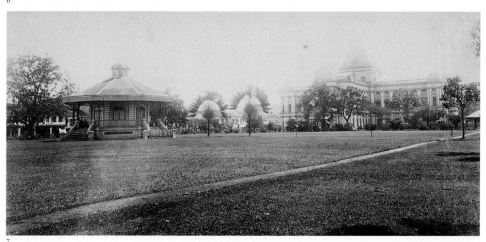

1

Malacca-born Tan Tock Seng (1798–1850) (2) arrived in Singapore in 1819 a vegetable seller. When he became one of the wealthiest merchants in the Straits Settlements, he did not forget the less fortunate. In 1844, he contributed the funds for a new paupers' hospital. The building, designed by John Turnbull Thomson (see pages 34–5), opened in 1849 amid desperate circumstances: among the Asian population poverty, malnutrition, overcrowding and opium smoking were rampant.

Unfortunately, the hospital (3) was a grim place from the start. It overlooked a dirt- and refuse-filled swamp. C. M. Turnbull records in *The Straits Settlements 1819–1867* a description by one Singaporean resident: '[it] was crowded with horribly diseased Chinese paupers, beggars and abandoned outcasts of all descriptions and in the last stage of disease and loathsomeness [where] the horrid sights around them and the foul air inside are most sickening and tend to bring on fever if not hospital gangrene.'

In 1857, the government acquired the building as a military store; by 1860 a new Tan Tock Seng Hospital was ready on Balestier Plain. After Tan Tock Seng's death, his son, Tan Kim Ching, became leader of the Hokkien Huay Kuan and the Kapitan China of the Straits Chinese community. The Seaman's Hospital and the Surgery (3) were also designed and built under Thomson's supervision.

3

4

2

5

Basic English education reached only a tiny minority during Singapore's first half century. Some small private schools came and went, usually collapsing after the demise of their founders, such as Reverend Benjamin Peach Keasberry (1811–75) who devoted his life to educating Singaporean Malays at his Malay College (9) in Kampong Glam. Father Jean-Marie Beurel (6) founded both St Joseph's Institution and the Convent of the Holy Infant Jesus in the 1850s, travelling to Europe to recruit teachers, and battling with the government to get land, building materials and funds. Miss Sophia Cooke (8) arrived in 1843 with the Society for the Promotion of Female Education in the East, and died in Singapore in 1894. She established Chinese Girls' School, now known as St Margaret's.

1 *Singaporean schoolboys, probably St Joseph's Institution, 1860s*
2 *Portrait of Tan Tock Seng*
3 *The original Tan Tock Seng Hospital, centre, between the Surgery and Seamen's Hospital at Pearl's Hill, John Thomson, watercolour, c. 1848*
4 *The Surgery, Pearl's Hill*
5 *Photograph of the new Tan Tock Seng Hospital, 13 February 1876*
6 *Father Jean-Marie Beurel, founder of St. Joseph's Institution and the Convent of the Holy Infant Jesus, early 1860s*
7 *View of the Convent grounds, 1860s*
8 *Sophia Cooke, pioneer in female education*
9 *Inscribed 'Malay College, Singapore', undated*

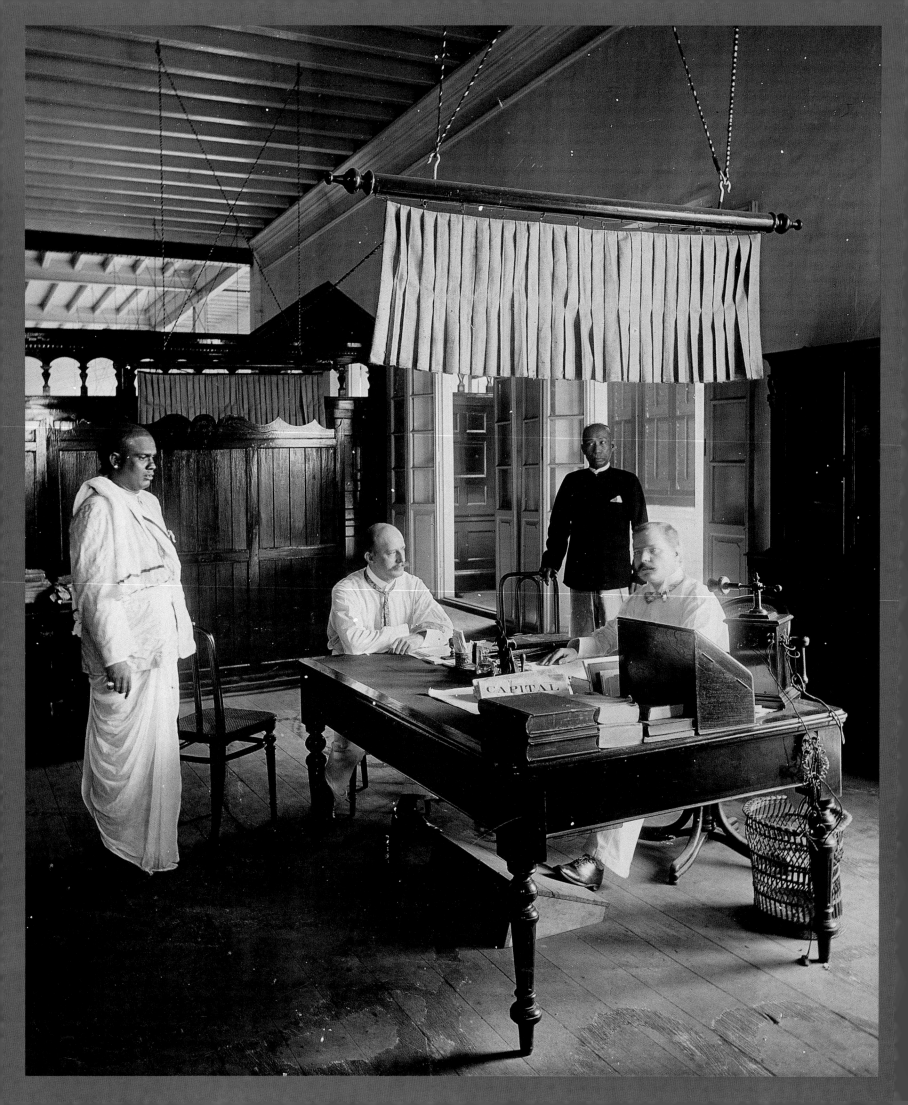

COLONIALS AND COOLIES
1870–1919

In April 1867, a young Dutch photographer by the name of G. R. Lambert placed an advertisement in the *Singapore Daily Times* 'to inform the community of Singapore, that he has this day opened a Photographic Establishment under the firm of G. R. Lambert & Co. in High Street, No. 1.' Mr Lambert then disappeared from Singapore, his return a full decade later, in May 1877, marked by a similar announcement. From that time on, until the end of World War I, the firm of G. R. Lambert & Co. faithfully recorded an era of buoyant expansion, stocking hundreds of large format original photographs (8 x 10 inches or 20 x 27.5 centimetres) of the topography and people of the island to sell to the public. It was the premier portrait studio and official photographer for all major political events. The world that G. R. Lambert & Co. photographed has long disappeared, the buildings demolished, the landscape altered, the style of living and dressing a distant memory, but the scenes captured with such skill are a remarkable album of the island a century ago. They form the backbone of this chapter.

Mr Lambert's first advertisement coincided with the year in which the Straits Settlements were placed under the administration of the Colonial Office, and his return with the increased importance of the port. This was the Singapore of colonials and coolies, the English *tuan besar* and the Chinese towkay and huge numbers of poor immigrants in search of a better life. Although new economic opportunities meant overnight fortunes for some, the vast majority struggled to survive. While the comforts of life improved for the wealthy, living conditions among the poor remained grim with the alarming spread of diseases caused by overcrowding, malnutrition and opium addiction. Although their importance as historical documents must not be underestimated, Lambert's photographs reflect a European bias, largely reinforcing an impression of steady growth while playing down the less savoury aspects of life.

The acceleration of Singapore's growth was fuelled by several factors. The opening of the Suez Canal in 1869 reduced travelling time between Asia and Europe by sparing ships the arduous journey around the southern tip of Africa. Then came the progressive conversion of sea travel from clipper ships to steamships. Singapore became one of the largest coaling stations in the world. Thousands of tons were shipped to the island. The Tanjong Pagar Dock

Company catered to 400 different customers, storing each coal pile separately in either wood and *attap* sheds or out in the open. The situation was less than ideal. After a disastrous fire broke out on the company premises on Friday, 13 April 1877, coal heaps were still smouldering two weeks later. The dirty work of coaling ships was done manually. Two by two, the coolies lugged the large baskets suspended from a thick bamboo pole between them, up one gang-plank, down another, back and forth, day and night.

Another factor was the extension of British protection to the Malay States where huge deposits of tin were discovered in 1848. A volatile combination of Malay dynastic disputes and feuding Chinese miners provided an excuse for intervention in 1874. After the murder in 1875 of James Birch, the first British Resident in Perak, the British strengthened their grip. In 1896, the Federated

ABOVE View from a jinrickshaw, c. 1909. Barefoot and bare chested, the jinrickshaw coolie ferried his passengers across the island for a few cents, enough to buy a hot meal and a sleeping bunk.
FACING PAGE Staff of the Singapore branch of Nederlandsche Handel Maatschappij (Netherlands Trading Society), one of the largest banking concerns in the world at the beginning of the 19th century, pose in their new premises at Nos. 1–2 Cecil Street in 1902, shortly after moving in.

Singapore was the crossroads of the East. The introduction of picture postcards enabled travellers to send favourite views of the city to friends and relatives back home.

Malay States was formed. This was the year in which 'Mad' Henry Ridley, Director of the Singapore Botanic Gardens and an enthusiastic supporter of the commercial development of rubber, received his first request for rubber seedlings. It came from Malaccan Chinese Tan Chay Yan, who converted one of his plantations to rubber. By 1919, Malaya had become the world's chief supplier of rubber, producing 50 per cent of the supply. It was also the world's single largest tin producer. Both commodities were brought to Singapore for shipping to the rest of the world.

Some the most dramatic changes to the island were those in and around New Harbour, formally renamed Keppel Harbour in 1900. Several companies carved facilities out of swamp and jungle, giving rise to the 'Liverpool of the East'. The most aggressive was the Tanjong Pagar Dock Company. It eventually swallowed up the competition, operating five dry docks and possessing a wharf frontage of 2 kilometres, together with warehouses for 200 000 tons of cargo and 250 000 tons of coal, and had properties spread over 150 hectares. But success proved a double-edged sword. The company was unable to finance improvements. In 1905, the colonial government acquired it and formed the Tanjong Pagar Dock Board. In 1912, the Singapore Harbour Board, the forerunner of the Port of Singapore Authority, was constituted.

When the submarine cable linking Singapore with Madras was laid in 1871, establishing direct telegraphic communication via India with Europe, the town was only slowly beginning to change. Fuelled by trade, immigrants and new wealth from tin and rubber, the pace accelerated decade by decade. The most dramatic projects were those along the waterfront: the massive reclamation of Telok

Ayer Basin in 1879–90, conceived to provide much needed road links between the town and the port; the extension of Collyer Quay to cope with traffic; and the reclamation of land in front of the Padang to form Connaught Drive. New public buildings were constructed, ranging from police and fire stations, markets and a general hospital, to a grand post office and a museum. As for the new generation of commercial buildings in Raffles Place and Collyer Quay, many were to last only a few decades before being replaced.

Distances decreased with the introduction of new modes of transport. Old fashioned horse-drawn gharries and bullock carts jostled alongside electric trams that covered a route of 25 kilometres end to end. The trams themselves faced stiff competition from jinrickshaws, introduced as public transport in 1880. The first automobile was imported in 1896, and by 1918 there were almost 1,800 motorized vehicles on the roads.

By 1900, travellers were routinely chronicling Singapore's stately business houses and banks, the iron pavilions shading the daily markets, the suburban roads embowered in lush greenery—and the racial composition of the population. Singapore's rising prosperity coincided with the last unsettled decades of the Qing Dynasty. As word of economic opportunities spread, thousands of Chinese immigrants flooded the shores. The immigrants from China were joined by Indians, Malays and many other races, all in search of fortune. In 1871, the population stood at 97,000 and by 1901 it reached 226,800. Europeans were a small minority. Amongst all races, men greatly outnumbered women.

Sir Harry Keppel (seated, centre) was called 'the father of the Harbour' because of his pioneering exploration of the area in the 1840s. He first came to Singapore in 1834 and made his last visit in 1903, when this photograph was taken.

The rising population put new pressures on the town, which began to grow beyond its tidy confines, encroaching on surrounding suburbs and swamps. The expansion began as ribbon developments along the main roads leading out of town: Tanjong Pagar, River Valley, Orchard, Bukit Timah, Thomson, Serangoon and Kallang Roads. The rise of 'automobilism' encouraged the building of new roads and residential areas in Katong, Siglap, Serangoon, Changi and the north. Wealthy Europeans and Asians enjoyed spacious villas in suburban districts near town. Toa Payoh, however, was still a farming district, Jurong a mass of mangrove swamps and the northern areas of the island covered by vast rubber plantations.

G. R. Lambert & Co. was by no means the only studio documenting the changing landscape. But their photographs are easy to identify because they dry-stamped their logo on the lower right-hand corner of each one. There were several other European-managed studios, such as the flamboyantly named ones with which George S. Michael was involved during a career running from the 1880s to around 1918: the American Lighting Gem Photographic Studio and the Celestial Studio being two. Moses and Co., later renamed The Standard Photographic Studio, was another enduring firm, with origins dating back to 1874. It closed at around 1917.

Towards the end of the century, Chinese studios proliferated. They concentrated on portraits, however, rather than topographical views. As early as 1861, one Lee Yuk from Canton advertised as a portrait painter, daguerreotype copier and photographer with premises at 139, Telok Ayer Street. Early Chinese photographers may have apprenticed with European photographers or learned the trade in missionary schools. The earliest known photographic manual in Chinese was published in 1873.

While the market for studio portraits continued well into the 20th century, the demand for large format topographical views dried up. After 1898, the market was flooded with mass-produced picture postcards, which were far cheaper to collect. European photographic firms were initially major players in the new trade, printing their stock images, but they soon faced stiff competition as Chinese professional photographers became involved in producing postcards. The growth of amateur photography was another factor. The complexities of early photography were such that special training was required. A series of innovations, culminating with the introduction of the Brownie camera in 1900, enabled anyone who could afford camera and film to take a snapshot. The efforts of several talented amateurs, such as E. W. Newell who lived in Singapore around 1909, are included in this

Queen's Scholars, 1886–8. This photograph appeared in Song Ong Siang's One Hundred Years' History of the Chinese in Singapore, written as part of the centenary celebration programme. Song (1871–1941) was a brilliant student who left Singapore for Britain in 1888 as a Queen's Scholar to study law. He was called to the English bar in 1893.

chapter. Their spontaneity form a striking, and pleasing, contrast to the formality of professional studio views.

Important events and occasions still called for the skills of the professional, and, as amateur photography was an expensive hobby, studios continued to do a brisk trade in portraits. The Japanese photographer M. S. Nakajima saw the potential, and first advertised around 1911 as 'photographer and artist'. Around the same time, Lee Brothers Studio opened in Hill Street. Cantonese brothers Lee King Yan and Lee Poh Yan belonged to a family of photographers, with several uncles already running studios in Chinatown. Their move from Chinatown into the Stamford Road area was almost certainly a move to attract a more diverse clientele. Here, the rich and aspiring, the famous and unknown, Chinese, Indian, Malay and European alike, went to the upper floor studio in search of that small bit of immortality in the form of the studio portrait. From this collection are drawn many of the portraits in this chapter.

1

2

At the beginning of the 19th century, the British ruled a quarter of the world's population and nearly a quarter of its land surface. Singapore was a jewel in the crown of Empire. By the time the Duke and Duchess of Cornwall and York arrived for a visit in 1901 (right), Singapore was considered an essential link in the chain of British ports and coaling stations, which stretched from Gibraltar through Malta, Suez, Aden, India and Ceylon (Sri Lanka), and on to Hong Kong and Australia.

During their hectic three-day visit, the royal couple lunched with several Malay Sultans, held a private interview with Tunku Ali, the descendant of the Malay chief who ceded the island to the British, dined at Government House and toured Chinatown by rickshaw, all duly recorded in *The Web of Empire*, a diary of the tour compiled by Assistant Private Secretary Sir Donald Mackenzie Wallace. The most significant event of the visit was the Durbar, a carefully choreographed function in the old Town Hall where the royal couple, grandly seated on their large dais, received tributes of loyalty from the various communities.

There were other royal visits, including that of Prince Arthur of Connaught in February 1906 (2). Receptions sometimes took the form of a garden party (1).

RIGHT The arrival at Johnston's Pier of the Duke and Duchess of York (the future King George and Queen Mary) on a three-day visit, 21–23 April 1901
1 Garden party, undated photograph, early 1900s
2 The newly completed Victoria Memorial Hall decorated for a royal visit, probably that of Prince Arthur of Connaught in 1906

Singapore became a Crown Colony in 1867, its rule officially transferred to the Colonial Office in London, along with that of Malacca and Penang which altogether formed the Straits Settlements. Loyalty to Empire was expressed in events such as the unveiling of the statue of Sir Stamford Raffles (4) in 1887. Regional visitors included the young Siamese King Chulalongkorn (1) and various Malay sultans (2). It, however, was the visits of the revolutionary Dr Sun Yat Sen (3) that sparked the imagination of the Chinese. He established a branch of his Tung Ming Hui, on 2 February 1906, at Wan Ching Yuan, Teo Eng Hock's bungalow.

FACING PAGE Visit of Prince Arthur, 1906
1 *Official visit of King Chulalongkorn in 1871, group photograph in the Singapore Botanic Gardens*
2 *Sultan of Selangor, Sir Abdul Samad, and followers at Government House, 27 March 1890*
3 *Visit of Dr Sun Yat Sen, photographed together with supporters of his Tung Ming Hui, c. 1910*
4 *The unveiling of the Raffles statue on the Padang on 27 June 1887 as part of Queen Victoria's Jubilee celebrations*
5 *The life-size portrait of Sir Frank Swettenham by John Singer Sergeant that commemorates his association with Victoria Memorial Hall*

Tin and rubber drove Singapore's prosperity, creating a class of enormously wealthy men and jobs for the masses of poor immigrants. The lure of wealth, the desire for control and great ambitions motivated British, Chinese and Malay alike, and shaped dramatic changes to Singapore's landscape.

In 1874, the British authorities embarked on a policy of intervention in the tin-rich Malay States, where Malay dynastic disputes and feuding Chinese miners were creating anarchy. To extend British influence, and protect British investments, British Residents were appointed as advisors to the rulers of Perak, Selangor and Sungai Ujong (in Negri Sembilan).

Tensions, however, seethed in Perak, where the Kinta Valley (2) was fast becoming the most important tin-producing district. James Birch, the first British Resident (1), proved arrogant, impatient and scornful of Malay customs and traditions. In November of 1875 he was murdered, speared by assassins while bathing. The British used this episode to tighten further their control and strengthen the Resident's authority.

By the end of the 19th century, Malaya was the world's single largest tin producer, thanks mainly to improvements in mining techniques and an increased demand for tin for tinned food and other consumer products. Tin smelting was one of Singapore's first modern industries. The Straits Trading Company, founded in 1886, built a tin smelter on Pulau Brani (3) in 1890 to smelt ore from Malaya.

Although the first rubber seedlings successfully arrived in Singapore in 1877, the commercial potential of rubber was largely ignored by Malayan planters who were enamoured with coffee. Indeed, the enormous enthusiasm of Henry Ridley, who arrived as Director of the Singapore Botanic Gardens in 1888 and quickly became convinced of its potential, earned him the nickname 'Mad' Ridley.

In 1896, Ridley received a request for seedlings from Malacca resident Tan Chay Yan, who planted 17 hectares on his plantation. The pace of planting soon quickened, stimulated by the invention of the pneumatic tyre and, of course, by the automobile. By 1919, Malaya was the chief supplier of rubber, producing half of the world's supply.

The first rubber trees in Singapore were planted in the final two years of the 19th century, and, as the crop caught on, hundreds of hectares were put under cultivation, stretching right across the northern part of the island. The rare photograph of seedlings (5) dates from the early 1900s. Seedlings took from five to six years to mature.

By 1920, much of the rubber cultivated in Singapore was controlled by Singapore-born Peranakan Lim Nee Soon (4), who was one of the first to capitalize on rubber's commercial potential. At one time, he controlled more than 8000 hectares of rubber trees in Thomson, Seletar, Sembawang, Jurong, Chua Chu Kang and Mandai as well as in Malaya.

---

1 British Resident of Perak, J. W. W. Birch (seated, far left) at Salak, Perak, November 1875, shortly before his assassination
2 Inscribed 'Open cast tin Mine, Kam Ting, Near Larut 1890'
3 Tin smelter, Pulau Brani, undated photograph, c. 1900
4 Lim Nee Soon visits his rubber estate, Singapore, photograph dated '11.11.1909'
5 Inscribed 'A rubber estate on opposite side of the road to the reservoir', early 1900s

4

5

1

2

3

4

The need for a railway, mainly to service the port, was discussed as far back as 1869, but only in 1899 was construction of the Singapore–Johor Railway authorized. The impetus was trade, and funds came from the government who was eager for a rail link with the tin-rich Malay States.

The formal opening of the Singapore–Kranji Railway took place on 1 January 1903. By April passengers could travel for an hour across 'some very pretty country' to the Bukit Timah Station. Several years later, the line extended from Keppel Harbour to the Woodlands terminus (4), where passengers disembarked and crossed to Johor by steam launch. The main passenger station was at Tank Road (facing page). Railway construction had been started in Perak (2 and 3) by the British, with the first section of 13 kilometres between Taiping and Port Weld opening in 1885. The extension of the system was stepped up after the Federated Malay States (FMS) was formed in 1896. In 1918, the properties and land of the Singapore Government Railway were sold to the FMS and incorporated into the FMS Railway (5).

FACING PAGE *Tank Road Station,*
c. 1910
1 *Railway Station, Malaya, c. 1910*
2 Inscribed 'Special train passing
the Marble Hill near Ipoh', 1890s
3 Inscribed 'Railway under
Construction, Taiping, 1892'
4 *Woodlands Station and jetty,*
c. 1910
5 *FMS Travel Guidebook, c. 1910*

5

1

2

The Tanjong Pagar Dock Company was established in 1864, when steamships and the impending completion of the Suez Canal were about to affect shipping and travel profoundly. Steamships needed deep-water wharf facilities and dry docks. Above all, however, they needed coal. Singapore's location, at the crossroads of East–West trade, made her one of the largest coaling stations in the world.

Of the handful of companies who built facilities at New Harbour, the Tanjong Pagar Dock Company was the most aggressive—and successful. By 1885, it controlled three-quarters of all wharf space (following pages). In 1899, after amalgamation with the New Harbour Dock Company, it controlled virtually the entire shipping business.

The expansion of the port stimulated enormous changes to the landscape. More roads, for example, were desperately needed to link port and town. Many major thoroughfares were created at this time. New Harbour Road, later Keppel Road, was laid across the mangrove swamps from Tanjong Pagar to Telok Blangah, and opened in 1886. The reclamation of Telok Ayer Basin (see page 112) permitted the formation of Anson Road, Cecil Street, Robinson Road and Raffles Quay.

More and better housing, offices and godowns were also required. European staff lived comfortably in large company bungalows (7 and 8), while seamen in transit could enjoy the facilities of the Boustead Institute (4 and 6) at the corner of Anson Road and Tanjong Pagar Road. Named after its main benefactor, Edward Boustead, who left a large sum of money to charity, it opened in 1892 on a site presented by the Tanjong Pagar Dock Company, and was funded by leading merchants. The building contained bedrooms, recreation rooms of various kinds and a hall for meetings.

3

1 Inscribed 'Coals at New Harbour', 1890s
2 Road near New Harbour, c. 1910
3 Inscribed 'Approach to Dock Premises', 1890s
4 Ground floor, Boustead's Institute, 1892
5 Inscribed 'Tanjong Pagar Police Station', 1890s
6 Inscribed 'Boustead Institute', Tanjong Pagar, 1890s
7 Inscribed 'Manager's Residence', 1890s
8 Inscribed 'Wharfinger's House', 1890s
9 Inscribed 'Entrance to Dock Premises', 1890s
10 Inscribed 'View of the Main Road', 1890s

FOLLOWING PAGES

RIGHT-HAND PAGE *View of the Wharf, 1890s*
1 Keppel Wharf, 1894
2 Inscribed 'Three Chinese Cruisers in Dock', 1890s

Ground Floor, Boustead Institute.

4

5

6

7

8

9

10

1

2

Machine-Shop, Tanjong Pagar Dock, Singapore.

1

2

3

4

SINGAPOUR Embarquement du charbon à bord d'un Paquebot
Liner Coaling

5

6

7

On the eve of its expropriation on 30 June 1905, the Tanjong Pagar Dock Company's facilities looked much as they had two decades earlier. Already there had been growing unease over the fact that the life of the port and, indirectly, the prosperity of the island, depended on the management of a single company.

In the 1890s, the company's extensive facilities included offices, machine shops (1) and godowns (3). All the wharves were supported on timber piers which rotted and had to be replaced every few years (4). While managers resided in airy bungalows, accommodation for port coolies was far less salubrious—in 1894, accommodation for some 1,740 port workers comprised nine sheds divided into cubicles. For years, one of the landmarks of the port area was the unsightly Cloughton's Hole (2), a remnant from the 1850s when an attempt to construct a dry dock ended in failure.

After the Singapore Harbour Board was constituted in 1912, it extended the port's limits and upgraded its facilities. The state-of-the-art King's Dock (7) opened in August 1913. Gradually, the entire wooden wharf frontage was replaced with concrete structures. New warehouses and cold storages were built, and the entire complex connected to the FMS Railway.

1 Inscribed 'Machine Shop, Tanjong Pagar Dock', 1890s
2 Inscribed 'Cloughton Hole', 1890s
3 Inscribed 'Interior of a Wharf Godown', 1890s
4 Inscribed 'Tanjong Pagar Dock under Construction', 1890s
5 Coolies loading coal the old-fashioned way, c. 1900
6 Officials of the Singapore Harbour Board, c. 1915
7 King's Dock, with Mount Faber in background, shortly after
   completion, c. 1915

1

2

3

4

5

8

6

7

Running the municipality was a complex and costly affair. The Municipal Ordinance of 1887 was a response to the growing need for a more sophisticated machinery to run the burgeoning city, and was patterned after the municipal authorities of British towns. It became responsible for shaping the urban environment. Water supply and fire control were major issues. MacRitchie Reservoir (5) had been open less than a decade before its capacity had to be increased and plans to build a second reservoir implemented—Pierce Reservoir opened in 1911. A Fire Brigade (4) was formed in the 1880s and three fire stations built. The opening of the Central Fire Station in 1909 led to a big drop in the number of fires.

Among the new generation of public buildings was the Police Court (3). By the 1890s, there were 30 police stations (1) across the island. The force included Europeans, Malays, Chinese, Sikhs, Tamils and a few Bengalis. A detective division (2) was set up at around 1900. To improve living conditions in Chinatown, back lanes were cut through some houses built back to back (8). The problem of opium was tackled by a high-powered commission (7) in 1907. Their report led to the government taking over the manufacture and sale of opium.

1 Police station interior, early 1900s
2 First Detective Branch, 1906
3 New Central Police Court, completed in 1885
4 Early fire station, 1890s
5 Opening of impounding reservoir at MacRitchie, 29 September 1894
6 The Municipal Commissioners, 1916
7 Opium Commission of the Federated Malay States and the Straits Settlements, 1907–8
8 Inscribed 'Cross Street During Demolition (of Back to Back Houses)' from the Singapore Municipality Report, 1915

1

5

2

6

3

4

7

8

9

Singapore's trade expanded eightfold between 1873 and 1914. Even with wharves at New Harbour, congestion on the River increased. While the port facilities handled long distance trade, smaller vessels and regional traders clustered around the mouth of the River. As tin and rubber fuelled the economy, larger premises were constructed by Chinese and European firms alike (1–3). River traffic improved with the completion of new bridges. The year 1886 saw the opening of both the new Coleman (8) and Ord Bridges. In 1889, Read Bridge was ready for traffic. At the mouth of the River, the old Cavenagh Bridge soon proved inadequate for the increase in traffic. Anderson Bridge finally opened parallel to it in 1909.

1 *Godowns at Clarke Quay, 1890s*
2 *Upper reaches of the River and Pulau Saigon, 1890s*
3 *North Boat Quay, 1890s*
4 *The upper reaches, 1890s*
5 *Lightermen and their boats on the River, 1880s*
6 *View of north Boat Quay, 1890s*
7 *Upper reaches with Ellenborough Market and* wayang *stage on the right*
8 *Elgin Bridge and Coleman Bridge under construction, 1886*
9 *Inscribed 'Rafting logs on the Singapore River', E. W. Newell, photographer, c. 1910*

1

2

It took more than a decade to reclaim Telok Ayer Bay (1). Traffic between the harbour and the River was heavy, and the extended seafront was desperately needed to improve road links between town and port. During the years that it took to complete the projects, goods were still carried on bullock carts along narrow roads in need of constant repair. By 1900, the situation had improved with the laying out on reclaimed land of Anson Road, Cecil Street, Robinson Road and Raffles Quay.

After the turn of the century, Collyer Quay (right) was deemed inadequate and extended to cope with increasing traffic. Many of the old buildings, which held the headquarters of the major trading and commercial firms, were replaced by new ones designed in the grand Edwardian manner. The Arcade, with its twin onion domes, was built in 1909 by the Alkaff family; Winchester House (in scaffolding) boasted an ornate Italianate facade; the grandest of all was the elaborate Hongkong and Shanghai Bank (2). So pronounced were the changes that a *Souvenir Guide to Singapore* published in the early 1900s noted, 'Singapore, architecturally, may well be proud of the many fine buildings which she possesses … Old buildings are continually being pulled down to give place to more elegant architecture. Her improvements in this respect are a certain forerunner of a great commercial future.'

RIGHT Collyer Quay and sea wall, c. 1910
1 The reclamation of Telok Ayer Basin after commencement in 1879, G. R. Lambert & Co., photographers
2 Collyer Quay and Hongkong and Shanghai Bank Building which was completed in 1877, G. R. Lambert & Co., photographers

1

2

3

4

5

6

7

Raffles Place (1 and 3) was the chosen location of banks, law firms and large businesses, although it retained for many years the hectic atmosphere of a marketplace. At the turn of the century, it was in a state of transition. A circa 1905 *Souvenir Guide to Singapore* described the square as presenting 'a rather medley appearance, half old, half up to date. Some of the ancient buildings yet remain, especially along the west side, standing cheek by jowl with others of most modern types and architecture. If the general aspect strikes one as incongruous, one cannot gainsay that it is interesting as affording a comparison with what the general appearance of Singapore was in early days and what it is now.'

Battery Road (2) was said to be the busiest of all streets. Widened at the same time as new buildings were constructed, it was lined with shops and showrooms, including the studio of G. R. Lambert & Co. In Fullerton Square, carriages and jinrickshaws gathered around the shaded Tan Kim Seng Fountain as patrons shopped or visited the Post Office or the Exchange Building, both also fronting the square (4). The Exchange Building was designed by the Superintendent of Public Works, William Daniel Bayliss, and opened in 1879. It housed the Singapore Chamber of Commerce and the Singapore Club. The new Post Office was completed to the design of the Acting Colonial Engineer Henry Edward McCallum in 1884. Long overdue, it was received enthusiastically by *The Straits Times*: 'The imposing external appearance of this immense building is equalled by its internal arrangement and ornamentation, showing that the architect has devoted a great deal of time and study and taken much pains with it.'

Other fin de siècle landmarks included *The Straits Times* Building in Finlayson Green (5), and Telok Ayer Market (7). The Nederlandsche Handel Maatschappij, or Netherlands Trading Society, Building, (6) was typical of the first generation of buildings to appear along Cecil Street. The premises at Nos. 1–2, at the corner of D'Almeida Street, were bought in 1901 and occupied the following year. The interior is shown on page 90.

1 *Raffles Place showing premises of John Little & Co., G. R. Lambert & Co., photographers, late 1890s*
2 *Battery Road, showing premises of G R Lambert & Co., photographers, late 1890s*
3 *The Dispensary Building at Raffles Place, c. 1905*
4 *The Exchange Building and the new Post Office shortly after its completion in 1884*
5 *Finlayson Green, showing the premises of* The Straits Times *at the end of Cecil Street, c. 1900*
6 *Nederlandsche Handel Maatschappij Building at Cecil Street, c. 1910*
7 *The new Telok Ayer Market, 1894*

1

2

3

Singapore's business community was remarkably cosmopolitan. British trading agencies and merchant houses, such as Alexander Guthrie & Co. (left), predominated. Founded in 1821, the company expanded their trading, banking and insurance interests in Singapore, while retired partners looked after interests in London. There were also Dutch, German, French, Italian and Scandinavian trading and insurance houses, banks and shipping lines. The Germans, in particular, were vigorous competitors until declared enemy aliens, and their properties seized at the outbreak of World War I.

LEFT *Undated photograph inscribed 'A. G. & Co. Godown, Singapore', probably Alexander Guthrie & Co., c. 1900*
1 *Singapore office of accountants McAuliffe, Davis and Hope, c. 1912*
2 *Office interior, unidentified location, c. 1910*
3 *Beneath the punkah fan, keeping cool before electricity was available, office interior, c. 1890*

1

2

3

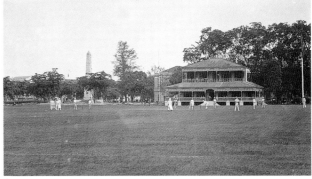

6

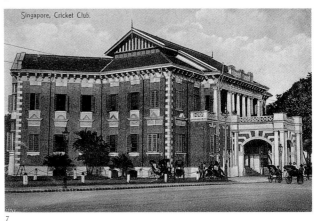

7

4

5

The civic quality of the Esplanade (1–3) was elevated and enhanced by the building of Victoria Memorial Hall where, on Singapore's centenary celebrations in 1919, the statue of Sir Stamford Raffles was relocated (4) from the Padang.

Following the death of Queen Victoria on 22 January 1901, a public meeting was held at which various ideas were put forward for a permanent memorial to her reign. It was decided that it should take the form of a public hall built adjacent to the existing Town Hall. Funds were raised largely by public subscription, as the committee in charge collaborated with both government and private architects to develop a suitably grand design. Victoria Memorial Hall officially opened on 8 October 1905; the 54-metre clock tower was finished the following year. To complete the ensemble, the Town Hall was almost entirely rebuilt. The retrofitting took four years but, upon completion in February 1909, the theatre (5) was considered on a par with any in London at the time.

Cricket had been played on the Padang from 1837, but it was not until around 1852 that a proper Cricket Club was formed; progressively grander clubhouses were built. The third clubhouse (6), completed in 1884, was given a face-lift in 1906–7 that involved adding wings to the pavilion which was refaced with bricks (7). The club, a European preserve, used half of the Padang at a peppercorn rental, while the other half was used by the Eurasian Singapore Recreation Club.

1 *The Esplanade and the third Cricket Club pavilion, 1890s*
2 *The Esplanade, A. L. Watson, painting, c. 1910*
3 *View of the Esplanade and harbour, A. L. Watson, painting, c. 1910*
4 *Centenary Day, 6 December 1919, and the unveiling of the statue of Sir Stamford Raffles in front of Victoria Memorial Hall*
5 *Victoria Theatre and the performance of* Here's Fun! *by the Singapore Amateur Dramatic Committee in aid of the Officers' Families' Fund, 1918*
6 *The third Cricket Club pavilion erected in 1884*
7 *The enlarged Cricket Club designed by Swan & Maclaren, 1906–7*

Vue de l'intérieur, John Little & Cie.   INTERIOR VIEW, JOHN LITTLE & Co.'s PREMISES   Innenansicht, John Little & Co.

1

Verreries et porcelaines, John Little & Cie.   GLASSWARE AND CROCKERY ROOM,   Glas- und Töpferwaren-Abteilung,
JOHN LITTLE & CO.   John Little & Co.

2

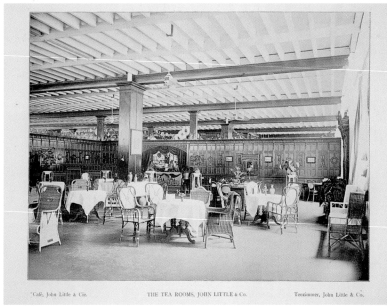

'Café, John Little & Cie.   THE TEA ROOMS, JOHN LITTLE & Co.   Teezimmer, John Little & Co.

3

Bijouterie et Argenterie, John Little & Cie.   SILVER WARE DEPARTMENT,   Silberwaren-Abteilung, John Little & Co.
JOHN LITTLE & Co.

4

High Street (6 and 7) and Raffles Place developed as the two premier shopping areas. John Little & Co. in Raffles Place traced its roots to the 1845 partnership of John Martin Little and Cursetjee Fromerzee, a Parsi. This partnership ended in 1853, but the business continued. A new store, designed by Swan & Maclaren and described as 'a very light and free Renaissance style, based on a study of Spanish and Flemish work', opened in 1910 (1–5). Shoppers could easily move between the two areas after the first jinrickshaws (8) were imported from Shanghai on 16 February 1880. By 1907, there were 7,469 jinrickshaws plying the streets, of which 998 were first class (with rubber tyres) and the remainder second class (with iron tyres).

1 *Interior view of the new store*
2 *Glassware and crockery room*
3 *The tea rooms*
4 *Silverware department*
5 *John Little & Co., the 'Universal Providers of Singapore' after the rebuilding of their Raffles Place premises, c. 1910*
6 *High Street from Fort Canning, 1890s*
7 *Hotel de l'Europe and High Street, 1890s*
8 *The jinrickshaw, 1880s*

Dépôt universel de Singapour.   THE "UNIVERSAL PROVIDERS" OF   Ein großes Warenhaus.
SINGAPORE.

5

31. View of High Street from Ft. Canning

6

Hotel del Europe and High St. S'pore.

7

8

B y the 1880s, Singapore boasted eight major hotels. The largest and best known was the Hotel de l'Europe (2 and 4). Established in 1857 in two old bungalows, it was entirely rebuilt in the early 1900s. Its greatest asset was its location at the corner of High Street opposite the Padang. The other hotels were clustered nearby. The Adelphi Hotel, established in 1863, was rebuilt around 1900 (5) boasting a dining room that seated 400 (3). The Hotel Van Wijk (1) was popular with Dutch travellers and famous for its tiffin curry. The Hotel de la Paix (6) occupied G. D. Coleman's old house in Coleman Street.

Raffles Hotel opened modestly in 1887. Under the founding Armenian Sarkies brothers, the property expanded steadily and its reputation spread. The main building (facing page), completed in 1899 to the design of Swan & Maclaren, marked the turning point from hostelry to grand hotel. The ground floor was given over to a 'Grand Marble Saloon capable of seating 500', where one dined under the comfort of whirring fans.

FACING PAGE *Main building, Raffles Hotel, completed in 1899 and*
   photographed c. 1911
1 *Tiffin Room, Hotel Van Wijk, Lee Brothers Studio, photographers, c. 1915*
2 *Verandah of Hotel de l'Europe, c. 1908*
3 *Tiffin Room, Adelphi Hotel, c. 1905*
4 *Grand Hotel de l'Europe after its rebuilding in 1907, Lee Brothers*
   Studio, photographers
5 *Adelphi Hotel, completed c. 1900*
6 *Hotel de la Paix luggage label, c. 1905*

1

These photographs show the area around Stamford Road and
Fort Canning in the years before and after the turn of the
century, a time when the open canal along Stamford Road (6)
was still a favourite washing spot for Indian dhobies.

The red brick YMCA (1) was, from its opening in 1911, a
prominent Stamford Road landmark. The organization had
become active in Singapore in the 1890s, and was given land by
the government for a permanent home. Much of the space was
given over to classrooms for the teaching of subjects as varied
as shorthand, typing, mathematics, book-keeping, electrical
engineering and the science of sanitation. During World War II,
the building became notorious as the Eastern Branch of the
dreaded Japanese Secret Police, or Kempetai.

Teo Hoo Lye's grand house (2) at the junction of Orchard
Road and Dhoby Ghaut was amongst the flamboyant Chinese
mansions built by successful immigrants. The house, according
to his obituary, 'took over three years to construct and cost
over $300,000'. It was designed by Swan & Maclaren and
completed at around 1913. Teo, one of the founders of the
Chinese Chamber of Commerce, made a fortune in sago and
branched into the steamer business. Teo later turned the house
into an educational institution which, at the time of his death in
1933, had some 400 pupils. In 1939, the house was demolished
to make way for the Cathay Building.

Wesley Methodist Church (3) was completed in 1908. The
Masonic Clubhouse (4) was inaugurated on 2 July 1888. The
first Masonic Lodge opened in 1845, and for many years occupied one of the Coleman-designed bungalows facing the Padang.

Stamford Road (5) was lined with enormous shady trees.
The cast-iron gates to the grounds of St Andrew's Cathedral
are recognizable. The view looks north towards the junction
with North Bridge Road, with Raffles Institution (hidden) to
the right of the large trees. Along Coleman Street (7) were
several hotels, including the Hotel de la Paix (right-hand side).
Fort Canning Swimming Pool (8) was one of the earliest public
swimming pools.

1 Opening of the YMCA, Stamford Road, Lee Brothers Studio,
   photographers, 1911
2 Stamford Road and house of Teo Hoo Lye, c. 1910
3 Wesley Methodist Church, Fort Canning, after its completion in 1908
4 Masonic Lodge at the foot of Fort Canning, inaugurated 2 July 1888
5 Stamford Road, outside the grounds of St Andrew's Cathedral, c. 1890
6 Stamford Canal, near Raffles Institution, 1890s
7 Coleman Street, 1890s
8 Swimming pool, Fort Canning, Lee Brothers Studio, photographers

2

3

4

5

6

7

8

The Raffles Library and Museum, which opened on 12 October 1887, consisted of a single building surmounted by a dome (2 and 3), the lower floor housing a library, reading rooms and an office which also contained the curator's living quarters and a small museum above. Thirty years later, the institution had doubled in size. The library (4) held 30,000 volumes, with extensive collections concentrated on the Malayan region, embracing zoology, botany, geology, ethnology and numismatics.

The transformation was due to the efforts of Dr R. Hanitsch (6), the German-born scientist who arrived to head the institution in 1895 at the age of 35 and retired 24 years later, in 1919. Dr Hanitsch embarked on a major reorganization that included identifying and arranging the huge collection of zoological specimens. The Museum's reputation spread, and the number of visitors increased. An extension in the form of a parallel back block opened in 1907. This enlarged the exhibition space considerably, permitting the mounting of the whale skeleton (5) along with an array of animals and artefacts.

One of Dr Hanitsch's final contributions was his organization of a centenary heritage search in 1919. An appeal went out for portraits, pictures, maps and photographs, some of which may have made their way into this book.

1 Undated photograph inscribed 'Foundation Stone, New Museum, Singapore', c. 1884
2 Side view of the original building after its opening in 1887
3 Portrait of the Museum, c. 1900
4 The library, c. 1910
5 Museum displays, c. 1910
6 Director's office, c. 1900

1

2

3

4

5

6

1

At the turn of the century, the prime residential area extended from River Valley Road (3) through to Tanglin, Claymore and lower Bukit Timah. In a rare 1880s view, Orchard Road (1) retains a country lane atmosphere. After 1900, however, development intensified. Emerald Hill, for example, was divided into small plots for the construction of bungalows and residential terraces, and the old market (7) was enlarged (8). The town end of River Valley Road (3) is where E. W. Newell photographed his housemates wearing *tutup* (4), a white cotton jacket with a high collar, which was standard office attire.

1 *Corner of Orchard Road and Scotts Road, looking north towards Tanglin with the Orchard Road Police Station on the left, c. 1890*
2 *Town end of Orchard Road at Dhoby Ghaut, looking from Fort Canning to Government House, 1890s*
3 *Inscribed 'River Valley Road', c. 1909*
4 *Inscribed 'MacKay, Makinson and Walker coming up the hill in River Valley Road', E. W. Newell, photographer, c. 1909*
5 *The town end of Orchard Road, c. 1890*
6 *The railway bridge, Orchard Road, c. 1900*
7 *Orchard Road Market before renovation, c. 1900*
8 *Orchard Road Market after renovation, c. 1910*

2

3

4

5

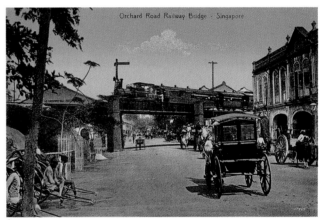

6

7

8

1

Life for the small European community was extremely comfortable. Under the chapter 'Social Life', the authors of the 1907 compendium *Twentieth Century Impression of British Malaya* noted, 'To the more prosaic, the charm will be found to lie in the material comfort with which he is able to surround himself. The European here usually occupies a more responsible position and commands a higher salary than at home, and, even after allowing for the difference in the purchasing power of money, this places within his reach many luxuries which previously he has been unable to enjoy. Added to this, there is the camaraderie engendered by the sense of expatriation and an absence of restraint ...'

Within the European community men vastly outnumbered women. Many bachelors preferred the camaraderie and economy of joining a mess, whereby they shared a bungalow and living expenses (4, 5 and 9). At home, the sarong (1 and 5) was widely worn and appreciated for its coolness and comfort. For women, jackets, corsets, linen and laces, heavy jackets and stylish hats were essential for formal outings. Even the Catholic nuns (8) retained their full habit while enjoying tea at the beach.

2

3

1 *Colonial bungalow, location not identified, undated, c. 1900*
2 *Family carriage ride, 1890s*
3 *Inscribed 'Stables at Burn Brai', 1890s*
4 *Bachelors at home, c. 1900*
5 *Inscribed 'Wilton, Lenthall, Douglas, Donal and Robinson, Indoor Dress Sarong and Singlet', E. W. Newell, photographer, c. 1909*
6 *Music room, c. 1910*
7 *Tea party, c. 1910*
8 *Nuns relax by the sea, c. 1920*
9 *Relaxing with the papers, c. 1900*

4

5

6

7

8

9

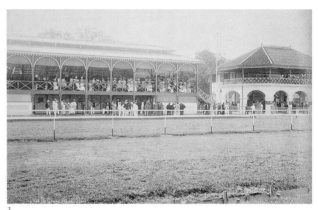

At the end of the 19th century the Indian community was scattered, with several distinct enclaves. Chulia and Market Streets had a concentration of South Indian Chettiars, small shopkeepers and labourers who worked along the river. High Street had attracted Sindhi, Gujerati and Sikh cloth merchants while Arab Street had Indian–Muslim textile and jewellery merchants. The port area had a concentration of Tamil, Telagu and Malayali workers. And then there was Serangoon Road.

Serangoon Road (1) was one of the earliest roads across the island. The Indian character of the town end of the road evolved gradually as it was close to the old Convict Jail, which closed in 1873, and had an abundance of water (2) which made it attractive to dhobies (4), as well as others involved in uniquely Indian activities such as dairying and tanning. It was also near the Racecourse (3) which offered employment opportunities.

1 *Serangoon Road, undated photograph, c. 1890*
2 *Rochor Canal, 1890s*
3 *The Racecourse at Farrer Park after rebuilding in 1904*
4 *Indian dhobies, 1890s*

1

2

3

4

5

6

7

Although Singapore ceased to be a convict settlement in 1873, Indian labourers continued to play a crucial role in the creation of the island's infrastructure. It was mainly Tamil labourers who laid the electric cables (1), built and repaired the roads (2 and 6), tapped the island's rubber trees (7) and laid the tramway tracks (4). Singapore Electric Tramway was registered as a company in London in 1902. Soon afterwards some 40 kilometres of track were laid, covering a route that ran 25 kilometres. Trams faced stiff competition from jinrickshaws, and fares had to be kept lower to compete.

1 Inscribed 'Laying electrical cables, Singapore', postcard, c. 1910
2 Road under repair, c. 1910
3 Sri Mariamman Temple, 1890s
4 Singapore Electric Tramway workers at North Bridge Road, 1904
5 Tamil-driven bullock carts transported goods at Boat Quay and the Port. Bullock-drawn water carts plied the streets, using water to keep down dust raised by vehicles.
6 Tamil coolies repairing road at the Chartered Bank Building, c. 1900
7 Tamil tappers, rubber estate, Malaya, c. 1910

1

Complex and crowded, Chinatown was a mosaic of coolie quarters, bazaars, theatres, shops and brothels. Between 1871 and 1931, Singapore's population increased from less than 100,000 to over half a million, due to the huge influx of immigrants. Most Chinese immigrants, or *sinkeh*, arrived indebt to a *kongsi* for their passage, but with the understanding that, after a designated period, they were free to seek employment elsewhere. The system was open to huge abuse. In 1877, the colonial government opened the Chinese Protectorate, with William A. Pickering, the first European official who could read and speak Chinese, as head. After tackling the abuses of the coolie trade, he moved on to secret societies and brothels, founding the Po Leung Kuk, or Office to Protect Virtue, to prevent forced prostitution.

1 China Street, early 1900s
2 Street in Chinatown, 1880s
3 Hokien Street, early 1900s
4 Inscribed 'Street in Chinese Town', early 1900s
5 Chinatown shophouses, 1890s

2

3

4

5

1

2

The architecture of Chinatown ranged from the basic and
utilitarian to the highly elaborate, such as the Chinese tea
house (5) and the extraordinary terraces (following pages).
Most buildings adhered to well-established southern Chinese
traditions in space planning, materials and architectural and
decorative details. The buildings were inevitably narrow and
deep—and a source of serious health problems.

In 1906, Professor W. J. Simpson, an expert in tropical
medicine, was commissioned to investigate the reasons for
Singapore's high death rates. He observed that, although the
city had inherited a legacy of orderly arrangement as a result
of Raffles' foresight in town planning, these advantages were
overshadowed by the Chinese practice of building over any
available space. In his report, published in 1907, Professor
Simpson wrote that shophouse extensions (added horizontally
rather than vertically) obstructed light, air circulation and 'the
efficient scavenging and drainage of houses'. The situation
was further aggravated by the tendency to divide floors into
cubicles which were filthy and overcrowded. The sick breathed
the same air and shared the same space as the healthy. Thus,
diseases spread easily.

One major problem was night-soil management. Until the
1880s, the disposal of night soil from the town was in the hands
of Chinese syndicates, who organized both collection in wooden
buckets (9), and transfer to farms and plantations out of town.
The Municipal authorities took over that responsibility but
retained the bucket system, amidst heavy criticism. In 1911,
plans for a water-borne sewerage system were unveiled.
However, implementation was extremely slow. By 1920, only
2 per cent of houses in the Municipal area had been connected.

1 *A busy Chinatown corner, c. 1900*
2 *Telok Ayer Street, 1890s*
3 *Near Market Street, 1890s*
4 *Inscribed 'Pearl's Hill Road', 1890s*
5 *Inscribed 'Chinese Tea House', early 1900s*
6 *New Bridge Road, 1890s*
7 *The durian seller transports his wares in baskets on his back*
8 *Opium smoking was a popular pastime amongst coolies*
9 *Night-soil carriers were a common sight*
10 *A shop front in Chinatown, c. 1890s*

FOLLOWING PAGES
Chinese shophouses, 1890s

3

4

7

8

5

WATER CARRIERS, SINGAPORE

9

6

10

1

2

Chinatown's residents were generally organized according to race and dialect, partly because of the original settlement pattern dictated in Raffles' 1822 Town Plan, and partly because of the tendency of new arrivals to gravitate towards an established support network, comprising relatives and family members, religious and clan-based welfare institutions and trade and occupational guilds.

Throughout Chinatown, much of life was lived on the street. Towards the end of the 19th century, advances in photography improved the camera's ability to capture street life. While the dramatic Chinese opera scene along the Singapore River (facing page) was professionally taken by G. R. Lambert & Co. in the 1890s, the market scene (1) and itinerant Chinese barber (2) are the work of amateurs. Chinese street opera, or *wayang*, was a cheap and popular form of entertainment. Until the construction of theatres in Chinatown, performances were enacted on temporary wooden and *attap* stages.

FACING PAGE Chinese opera stage, near Ellenborough Market, Singapore River, 1890s
1 *At the market, a spontaneous moment caught on camera, c. 1910*
2 *Chinese barber grooms queues, the pigtails imposed by the Qing rulers, c. 1910*

1

2

3

4

5

6

7

Amongst the early enthusiastic practitioners of amateur photography was E. W. Newell, whose albums, circa 1909, were donated to the National Archives of Singapore. Several of Newell's images are shown in this chapter, including the Chinese wedding procession (2). Chinese women were still relatively few in Singapore after the turn of the century, and the novelty of a wedding procession caught the attention not only of the photographer, but also of pedestrians along the road, such as the gentleman on the left.

Although Chinese communities eventually built places of worship all over the island, none was as large or as lavish as Siong Lim Temple (5). It was modelled after Xi Chan Shi, a famous temple in Fujian Province, with which it continued to retain a relationship. Both are rare examples of *cong lin* temples. The term, which means 'layers of forest', was used to describe a style of monastery whereby the physical arrangement consisted of seven functional halls. Besides Xi Chan Shi, there are four other major cong lin temples in Fujian Province.

The temple was built on land that was part of a tract of 15 hectares purchased by wealthy Fujian businessman Low Kim Pong (1838–1908) (7) in 1895. Construction was carried out in phases, with Low donating the largest single amount of funds. The official founding date of the temple is given as 1898, although the buildings were completed only in 1912.

Symmetrical in plan, the buildings are arranged along a central axis, separated by courtyards and orientated in a north–south direction, with the entrance facing south according to the principles of *feng shui*. The temple became a popular destination for school excursions (4) as well as for visitors from abroad (5).

---

1 Lantern Festival, c. 1910
2 Inscribed 'Chinese Wedding Procession', E. W. Newell, photographer, c. 1909
3 Priest and acolyte, Thian Hock Kheng temple, 1890s
4 Inscribed 'Temple at Kim Keat Road. Visit by the Gan Eng Seng School', 1920s
5 Monks and visitor, Siong Lim temple, c. 1910
6 Temple roofs
7 Low Kim Pong, c. 1907

The Malay population still congregated in the kampongs on the northern edge of the city, living in wooden and *attap* houses on poorly drained land fringing the tidal swamps around Kallang and Rochor Rivers. The location of Sultan Mosque in Kampong Glam, one of several distinct kampongs, remained a powerful focus for the Malay–Muslim community. Boat-building (3) was an important economic activity. Nearby Tanjong Rhu (6 and 7) was described as a 'lethal combination of shipping, kampongs, sawmills and oil stores'. Malay communities in the vicinity of the port area (4 and 5) were affected by both port expansion and the opening of new roads, such as Keppel (New Harbour) Road in 1886. The family portrait (2) was snapped in Changi.

1 *Young Malays with bicycles, c. 1890*
2 *Inscribed 'A Malay Group at Changi', E. W. Newell, photographer, c. 1909*
3 *Kampong Rochor, G. R. Lambert & Co., photographers, 1890s*
4 *New Harbour Road (later Keppel Road), early 1900s*
5 *Road to New Harbour, 1890s*
6 *Wharf at Tanjong Rhu, 1890s*
7 *Malay sailing craft, Tanjong Rhu, early 1900s*

1

2

3

4

5

6

7

1

2

3

4

As the population increased, and land in established town areas rose in price, the East Coast became increasingly attractive as a residential area, although development remained gradual until after World War I. An 1892 *Guide to Singapore* described Tanjong Katong as 'a long beach above which small country bungalows peep through groves of coconut palms', a description that also aptly applies to the idyllic photograph of Siglap (5) taken around that time.

Initially, access was fairly difficult because of the lack of roads linking the town with the East Coast. After the turn of the century, however, the area became increasingly popular with wealthy Straits Chinese who built bungalows along the shore as weekend retreats or second homes. Some of the properties also boasted swimming enclosures.

The Singapore Swimming Club (4) opened on 5 February 1894, and more than 10 years later members were still conveyed by launches between the club and Johnston's Pier (3). Among the European community, the club was considered the 'chief Sunday morning resort of young men.'

Seaview Hotel (2) opened in a coconut grove in 1906 with 40 rooms, a beer garden, tennis courts and a swimming enclosure. Another landmark was Geylang Police Station, near the junction of Paya Lebar and Geylang Roads (7). The location of the *kedai* (6) is not known, but it is from an 1890s family album together with the other views of the East Coast.

---

1 Malay women, E. W. Newell, photographer, c. 1909
2 Seaview Hotel, early 1900s
3 Inscribed 'From Launch to Club House in sampan', E. W. Newell, photographer, c. 1909
4 Singapore Swimming Club which opened on 5 February 1894
5 Tanjong Siglap, G. R. Lambert & Co., photographers, 1890s
6 Kedai kopi, probably near Bedok, 1890s
7 Changi Police Station, G. R. Lambert & Co., photographers, 1890s

ng Seglap. 24b

5

6

7

of Mount Palmer.
S.pore.

1

2

3

6

7

4

5bs. Road to Bukit Timah Bungalow.

5

The location of many of these rustic scenes can be identified with certainty thanks to G. R. Lambert & Co.'s habit of etching a caption onto the glass-plate negative. While the road at Bukit Timah (5) may bear some semblance to the landscape near Bukit Timah Hill at the end of the 20th century, all of the other places have changed beyond recognition. Chancery Lane (4) was a palm-lined dirt road when this photograph was taken in the 1880s, as was Bukit Timah Road (3), where as late as 1892 traces of tigers were still occasionally found.

The area around the base of Mount Palmer (1) was eventually altered to accommodate the growth of the port, but, until then, its beach was a pleasant alternative to the crowded streets of nearby Chinatown. The precise location of the Chinese village (2) is unknown, but its timber and *attap* buildings were probably similar to those built by Singapore's earliest rural Chinese inhabitants. Such villages were to be found along the major roads out of the town including Bukit Timah Road, Thomson Road and Serangoon Road. Tanglin Road (7) was a country track at the turn of the century. Further from town, a rubber estate at Seletar (6) was photographed in 1918.

1 Inscribed 'Foot of Mount Palmer', 1890s
2 Chinese village, possibly at Bukit Timah
3 Bukit Timah Road, 1880s
4 Chancery Lane, 1880s
5 Inscribed on the reverse in pencil 'Road at Bukit Timah, Singapore, A Tiger Resort', 1890s
6 Inscribed 'A rubber estate at Seletar Road, 1918'
7 Tanglin Road, G. R. Lambert & Co., photographers, 1890s

1

Before virtually all available agricultural land was given over to rubber trees, tapioca was cultivated on huge tracts in the latter half of the 19th century. The crop was popular with Chinese farmers, and it was also one of the staples of Trafalgar Estate at Seletar where, in 1880, there were about 400 hectares planted in tapioca. A large album in the Singapore History Museum contains a dozen views of the estate by G. R. Lambert & Co., which document the planting and processing of the crop (4–6). However, tapioca exhausted the soil, which then took as long as 15 years to recover. The abandoned tapioca plantations turned into huge stretches of *lalang* and brush, which fortuitously recovered just in time to be planted with rubber.

The sago palm (3) was only ever grown in Singapore in small quantities, mainly because it took some 12 years to mature. The last plantation of the palm (from which sago flour is made) was in Changi where a small business was carried on.

Pineapple tinning was a major industry at the turn of the century. The pineapple plant was a common sight in rubber estates as it was grown between the rubber trees, and could bear fruit and reap profits during the five to six years it took for the rubber trees to mature. Lim Nee Soon (1) was dubbed the 'Pineapple King'. He cultivated pineapples on his estates and operated a pineapple tinning factory near Syed Alwi Road.

2

3

1 *Lim Nee Soon visits his pineapple plantation, April 1916*
2 *Inscribed 'Dressing rattan, Singapore'*
3 *Sago manufacturing, 1890s*
4 *Inscribed 'Tapioca Grinding from an album depicting planting and processing of tapioca on the Trafalgar Estate, Singapore', 1880s*
5 *Inscribed 'Tapioca Flour and Pearls', from the same album*
6 *Inscribed 'Tapioca Washing Vats', from the same album*

4

5

6

At the end of the 19th century, Singapore was the economic and cultural hub of the Malay–Muslim world in Southeast Asia, a focus for regional trade and immigration and a publishing centre for Muslim religious writings and journalism. With the advent of steamships, Singapore also became the centre for the Mecca pilgrim trade.

The Malay population increased from less than 12,000 in 1869 to more than 22,000 in 1881, to 36,000 in 1901. By 1892, there were 23 mosques on the island. The community was enriched by immigrants from Riau, Sumatra, Java, Baewan, Sulawesi and other islands, and included Arabs and the English speaking Jawi–Peranakans. The first Malay language newspaper in the region, *The Jawi–Peranakan*, was published in Singapore in 1876. Community leaders included the wealthy Alsagoff and Alkaff families. The Alkaffs' farewell gathering at their residence in 1916 for R. J. Wilkinson, author of the *Dictionary of the Malay Language* (3), was recorded for posterity.

The subjects in the studio portraits are unknown; the photographs are from Lee Brothers Studio which operated in Hill Street from about 1910 to the mid-1920s. They show how the sitters looked when they sought to make an impression with their wealth and dignity. In contrast, the portraits of Koran reading (1), the Malay orchestra (4) and the postman (12) are 'character types' of the kind sold to tourists. The inscribed photograph of musicians (2) is from an 1890s family album.

1

Our Sunday visitors down at Tanjong Katong.

2

154

3

5

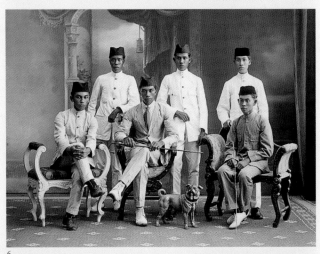

6

7

4

8

9

10

11

12

1

2

3

4

5

8

6

7

In 1871, Singapore's Indian population reached 11,501, and, by 1901, had risen to over 16,000. Though relatively small, it was composed of immigrants from all the major ethno-linguistic groups of the Indian subcontinent. Singapore was no longer a penal colony after 1873, when all Indian convicts still under sentence were relocated to the Andaman Islands. South Indians formed the largest community. Labourers from South India formed the core of the workforce that built the island's infrastructure—laying electricity cables and tramlines, and building and maintaining roads.

However, the studio portraits here, of unknown families and groups from the Lee Brothers Studio collection, portray the more affluent segments of the community: the successful merchants, civil servants and rising professionals. Indians were involved in a wide range of economic activities. Merchants were conspicuous as textile and jewellery traders, retailers and moneylenders. Their businesses were scattered across town, from Raffles Place to High Street and Arab Street.

Educated Indians became more visible in the British administrative machinery, filling subordinate posts in the

9

medical, education and police departments. Both missionary and government schools were staffed almost wholly by Indians. The police force was virtually dominated by Sikhs (8) and Tamils. The small number of Indian women (1) generally stayed at home. Those in the workforce were mostly teachers, attendants, nurses and doctors.

Towards the end of the 19th century, several Chinese photographers opened studios in Singapore. The studio—Pun Loon at High Street, Poh Wah at Upper Chin Chew Street, Tien Seng at North Bridge Road, and Kwong Sun, Koon Hin and Guan Seng along South Bridge Road—printed their names on the backs (1) or fronts (9) of the cardboard mounts.

Portraits have a long-standing importance in Chinese culture, the most common example being traditional ancestral portraits. Initially, Chinese photographers followed the conventions of the painter in presenting a formally garbed sitter in a static seated pose (2), and only gradually moving towards a more naturalistic approach (3, 4 and 5). The use of props was common. It was usual to include a small table, and to place on it some combination of flower vases or potted plants, teacups, books, pipes or clocks. Photographs from this period record the dramatic changes in conventions of hair and dress that took place at the end of the Qing Dynasty.

Among the proponents of the naturalistic style was Lee Brothers Studio (3, 4, 5, 7 and 8), which was run by Lee King Yan and Lee Poh Yan at Hill Street in the early 1920s.

2

3

1

4

5

6

7

8

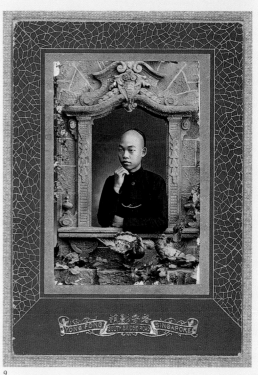

9

1

2

There was a gradual
increase in the number
of Chinese female immigrants
to the Straits Settlements.
The ratio of women to men
increased from 20 per cent in
1901 to 26 per cent in 1921,
to 38 per cent in 1931.
Weddings (4) and births (5–8)
became common affairs,
although the infant mortality
rate was high.

The early years of the 20th
century also saw an increase
in the number of social clubs.
The Amateur Drawing
Association was formed in
September 1909. In 1913,
they held an exhibition at the
Aldephi Hotel and hosted a
reception at Lee Choon Guan's
residence, Mandalay Villa, for
the Chinese ambassador to
France and Spain (2).

This was the era of grand
houses such as Golden Bell
(3), built by Tan Boo Liat as
his residence in Pender Road
in 1909. He was a supporter
of causes old and new, from
the Thian Hock Kheng Temple
to the Singapore Chinese Girls'
School and the Revolution in
China. When Sun Yat Sen
returned from America and
Europe to China in the wake
of the 1911 Revolution, he
stopped at Singapore and
spent the night at Golden Bell.

The fragment (9) shows
the Reverend J. A. B. Cook
with some of his young
congregation in the 1890s.

3

4

5

6

7

8

9

Lim Boon Keng (1) described the Chinese Peranakans as 'a new race created by the fusion of Chinese and Malay blood'. Lim (1869–1957) was a Queen's Scholar who bridged the Chinese and British worlds in a unique way. The founder of Singapore Chinese Girls' School, he was an advocate of female education, promoting policies for girls, such as the granddaughters (2) of the Teochew towkay Tan Yeok Nee.

The majority of Singaporean Chinese were China-born, but a handful of Straits Chinese leaders commanded disproportionate influence. One of the most prominent 'King's Chinese' was Tan Jiak Kim (1859–1917) (3), an English-educated community leader and one of the founders of the Straits Steamship Company.

Lim Nee Soon was raised by his grandmother (5). Tan Keong Saik was one of the early advocates of education for girls. He arranged for Miss Sophia Blackmore to give his daughters (7) English lessons.

Lee Cheng Yan (1841–1911) posed with his son Lee Choon Guan and grandchildren (6). Lee was a community leader and a successful businessman, often dealing with the European community. Lee Choon Guan followed in his father's footsteps.

7

8

9

10

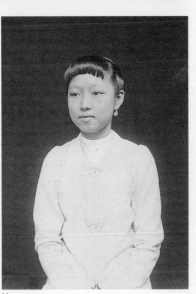

11

Singapore was a cosmopolitan city at the turn of the century, enlivened and enriched by small groups of Armenians (8), Jews, Japanese (9, 10 and 11), Europeans and Eurasians. The European community was small, steadily hovering at around 3,000 between 1880 and 1900.

The Eurasian population expanded and settled mainly in the Katong area. They were a very mixed community, with people of Portuguese or Dutch extraction from Malacca as well as growing numbers of Anglo Indians and Anglo Chinese. Most spoke English as their mother tongue.

The most famous Jewish resident was Manasseh Meyer (5). He was born in India in 1846, completed his education in Singapore, invested wisely in property, served as a Municipal Commissioner in 1893–9, was knighted in 1900 and built the Chased-el Synagogue in 1905.

The first Japanese in Singapore were young girls sold into prostitution. By 1890, there were over 100 girls in brothels. The Japanese Consulate opened in 1889, and the Japanese mercantile and professional community began to expand. Japanese doctors and dentists found a good clientele. In 1912, a Japanese elementary school opened; in 1915 the Japanese Association was formed.

2

3

4

5

6

1

7

8

9

10

11

While the discomforts of life lessened for the wealthy, living conditions among the poor were grim. The rampant spread of endemic diseases such as beriberi, tuberculosis, dysentery, malaria and enteric fever were caused by poverty, overcrowding, malnutrition and poor hygiene, the same conditions which also encouraged cholera and smallpox epidemics. The high mortality rate—higher than in Hong Kong, Ceylon or India—was also attributed to opium addiction among the poor who could only afford to smoke opium dregs. This changed after 1910, when the government took over the production and sale of opium and stopped the sale of dregs.

Abandoned babies were often left outside the gates of the Convent of the Holy Infant Jesus, which housed an orphanage (2), a girls' school and a refuge for distressed women. Public donations were the main source of funds. Thong Chai Medical Institution was set up in Chinatown in 1867 to provide free treatment to the poor, and, in 1892, it was given land by the government for a new dispensary (1). Physicians from China were engaged to provide free consultation and treatment to all. Tan Tock Seng Hospital moved to new premises in Moulmein Road in 1909 (3 and 5).

A new General Hospital opened in 1882 (4), and Middleton Hospital, specializing in the treatment of infectious diseases, opened in 1907. Doctors were recruited from Britain and India until the opening of the medical college in 1905 (7).

1 Thong Chai Medical Institution, Wayang Street, 1890s
2 Abandoned children, Convent of the Holy Infant Jesus, early 1900s
3 Captioned 'Ward of the old Tan Tock Seng Hospital with mosquito curtains'
4 Captioned 'Men playing golf at Sepoy lines with General Hospital in the background', c. 1910
5 Tan Tock Seng wards
6 Singapore General Hospital medical staff, c. 1910
7 Opening of the Straits and Federated Malay States Medical School, 1905

1

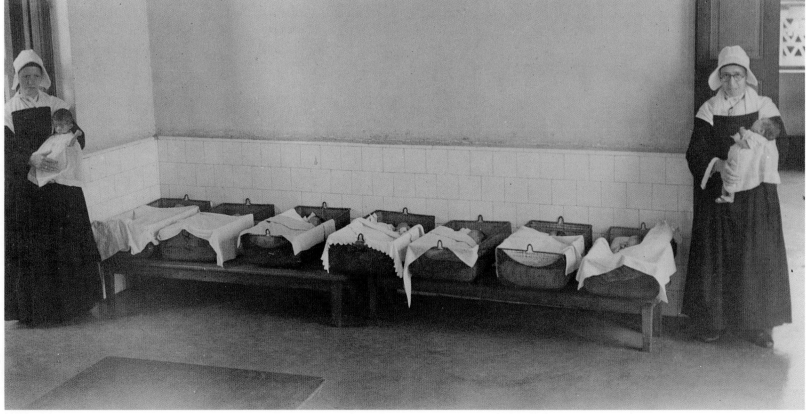

2

3

4

5

6

7

1

2

3

St. Joseph's Institution, Singapore.

7

The colonial government initially stayed largely aloof from educational issues, but subsidized the private English schools run by Christian missions and acknowledged a special responsibility for providing free vernacular education to Malays. A fundamental shift in policy occurred in 1902, when a special Education Commission recommended that the government establish English-medium primary schools. This set in motion a series of developments, including the setting up of an Education Board in 1909, and the doubling of places in English-medium schools between 1904 and 1911.

At the same time, changes occurred in Chinese education. At the end of the 19th century, there were more than 50 small, privately run Chinese schools teaching in dialect along traditional Confucian lines, but the standards were low. Influenced by educational reforms in China at the end of the 19th century, the Hokkien Huay Kuan established Tao Nan School in 1906, one of the first six 'modern' Chinese primary schools in Singapore. Classes were first held in the residence of Tan Kim Ching in North Bridge Road (3). After the 1911 Revolution, Tao Nan became the first Chinese school to change the language of instruction to Mandarin. The first Chinese-medium girls' school, Chung Hua Girls' School, opened in 1911.

The Methodist mission opened several schools, including Anglo-Chinese School in 1886, which moved into its premises at the foot of Fort Canning (5) in 1993, Fairfield Girls' School in 1889 (2) and Methodist Girls' School in 1888 (7). The early 1900s saw the expansion of the Convent of the Holy Infant Jesus and St Joseph's Institution (4).

The first non-Christian English-medium school for girls, Singapore Chinese Girls' School (1), was the brainchild of Dr Lim Boon Keng who struggled for years against the conservative Straits Chinese community. On the eve of the school's opening in 1899, he wrote in *The Straits Chinese Magazine*, 'The scheme, as was expected, met with a great deal of opposition and criticism, the bitterness of which only those who have worked so hard for its success, can speak fully.'

1 *Singapore Chinese Girls' School, early 1900s*
2 *Fairfield Methodist Girls' School, 1890s*
3 *Tao Nan School boys, c. 1905*
4 *St Joseph's Institution, c. 1910*
5 *Anglo-Chinese School, c. 1893*
6 *Chinese school boys with their queues cut, c. 1913*
7 *Methodist Girls' School, c. 1915*

CHAPTER 3

COSMOPOLITAN CITY
1920–1940

A mood of optimism and confidence filled the air as Singapore celebrated its centenary in February 1919. The Great War in Europe was over, the British Empire safe. Trade boomed with the healthy demand for goods following wartime shortages. Several projects were devised to permanently mark the crossing of this historic threshold. The founding of a college of higher education was the most ambitious, and this was achieved in 1928 with the opening of the Raffles College of Arts and Sciences. The celebrations also generated two official histories: *One Hundred Years of Singapore* told the story of the small British community, while *One Hundred Years' History of the Chinese in Singapore* was largely about the Straits Chinese. Yet, even as the authors compiled their tales of adventure and pioneers, there loomed serious social problems which were largely glossed over.

The centenary was followed by a decade of unequalled prosperity fuelled by global demand for rubber and tin. Much of the rubber was exported from Malaysia via Singapore to the United States of America where, in 1913, Henry Ford had introduced the first assembly line in his automobile factory in Michigan. The new production method lowered prices, turned the dream of a family car into a reality, and paved the way for a boom in rubber prices. Because Singapore had become so dependent on international trade, it was hard hit by the Great Depression. The price of rubber fell from an average of 34 cents in 1929, just before the Wall Street crash which triggered it, to a low of 4.95 cents in June 1932. It was a time of hardship for all Singaporeans. By the mid-1930s, the worst was over, but the fever pitch of prosperity never returned.

Up until then, prosperity continued to attract large numbers of immigrants. The growth in population, from 303,321 in 1911 to over half a million in 1931, was largely due to immigration, although there was a steady climb in the number of births, brought about partly by the gradual increase in the number of women, and partly by improvements in health care. The general worsening of the economy and the closure of some tin mines and rubber estates during the Depression led to widespread unemployment. In response, the government repatriated unemployed immigrants to China and India and, for the first time, imposed a quota on Chinese male immigrants, effective from 1 August 1930.

Governance of the island remained firmly in the hands of the British. At the top of the colonial pyramid was the Governor appointed by the Colonial Office in London. He ruled in consultation with the leaders of the European business community and with a tiny section of the wealthy, professional English-speaking Asian minority. Administration was carried out by the Malayan Civil Service, where top positions were reserved for British-born subjects of pure European descent on both sides, although British subjects of any race could apply for middle-ranking executive and technical posts. Only in 1932 was the Straits Medical Service opened to Asians. A Straits Civil Service was created in 1934 and a Straits Legal Service in 1937, to which Asian graduates from British universities could apply.

The trauma of World War I made the British acutely aware of the need to protect their Imperial interests on a global scale. Singapore was an obvious location for a stronger defence presence. In the early 1920s, plans were formulated for a massive naval base in the north of the island, between Sembawang and Woodlands, overlooking the Straits of Johor. Work on the mass of jungle, rubber trees and crocodile-infested mangrove swamp started slowly, but speeded up after the Japanese conquest of Manchuria in 1931. The naval base, built at a cost of £60 million, was formally opened in 1938, supported by additional military bases in Changi, Alexandra

FACING PAGE *Stamford Road decorated for the visit of the Prince of Wales in 1922.*
ABOVE *Early aviators at the Racecourse in Farrer Park shared the turf with horses. Singapore was a transit stop for many long-distance fliers, but its own aviation infrastructure developed slowly.*

Chroniclers of history. Charles Burton Buckley (1844–1912) lived in Singapore for nearly half a century. His Anecdotal History of Old Times in Singapore 1819–1867 *was published in 1902. Song Ong Siang (1871–1941) (second from left) was a fifth generation, Cambridge-educated Straits Chinese. His* One Hundred Years' History of the Chinese in Singapore *was published in London*

in 1923 as part of Singapore's centenary celebrations. The two-volume One Hundred Years of Singapore *was primarily the story of the small British community. Senior Editor Walter Makepeace (extreme right) was proprietor and editor of the Singapore Free Press. Co-editor Roland Braddell (second from right) was the third generation scion of a distinguished Straits family.*

and Ayer Rajah. By then, China was in chaos, occupied by the Japanese and torn between the Communists and the Kuomintang. Over Europe war clouds were gathering yet again.

During the boom years, the colonial government had increased spending on neglected areas, such as education and medical services. It also embarked on a building programme which saw the construction of a number of imposing civic landmarks: the Municipal Building (1929) (now City Hall), a new General Post Office, or Fullerton Building (1929), the Supreme Court (1939), the new Railway Station at Keppel Road (1932), Hill Street Police Station (1934), and Clifford Pier at Collyer Quay (1931). One important milestone was the completion of the Johor Causeway in 1923, linking Singapore with the Malayan mainland by road and rail.

Another milestone was the opening of Kallang Airport 15 years later, on 12 June 1937. The authorities had been slow to respond to the potential of commercial aviation. The first sighting of an aircraft was the demonstration flight by a Frenchman at the Farrer Park racetrack in 1911. In 1919, Captain Ross Smith piloted the first plane to land in Singapore, also at the racetrack, during his epic solo flight to win the first England-to-Australia air race. In 1923, the British government decided to construct a seaplane air base at Sembawang, near the proposed naval base, and a Royal Air Force base at Seletar. Work on the Seletar Aerodrome commenced in 1927, the same year that Charles Lindbergh made his solo nonstop flight across the Atlantic, from New York to Paris. Strides were

also made in organizing the routing of planes for carrying air mail, the speedier postal and newspaper services bringing Singapore into closer contact with world affairs. Yet, passenger traffic was still a secondary consideration. Construction on Kallang Airport started only in 1932, and took five years to complete. By then, Singapore was already a popular stopover for flights from Europe to the Far East (they landed at Seletar). By the late 1930s, there were daily flights to Kuala Lumpur, Ipoh and Penang.

The task of running the town was in the hands of the Municipal Council, which faced a considerable challenge in improving services. Far larger quantities of water were being consumed because of new factories, new suburban districts, a busy port and a growing population. In 1920, the Water Engineer recommended that a new supply of water be sourced in Johor and piped to Singapore. A site at Gunong Pulai, some 32 kilometres northwest of Johor Bahru, was selected. An impounding and pumping station was built at Seletar, where the first supply was received in 1932.

Electricity was becoming a necessity rather than a luxury. The first public power supply had come from the power station built by the Singapore Tramway Company in the early 1900s at MacKenzie Road to run its electric trams. The company and the Council entered into an arrangement to distribute some of the electricity to a handful of private consumers. But it was not until 1922 that electricity was supplied to selected suburbs, including Tanglin. With demand fast outpacing supply, a site for a new municipal power station was chosen on Cape St James, and it was officially commissioned in March 1927. An electricity showroom was opened on Orchard Road where a scheme for the hiring of electric fans and domestic appliances was introduced. The number of consumers connected to the power supply network rose from 1,452 in 1920, to 13,100 in 1930, reaching 28,255 in 1939.

One of the most far-reaching changes during this period was the increase in people's mobility, as the car emerged as an affordable and reliable means of transport. Mass production had brought prices within reach. To cope with the increased traffic, old roads were widened and resurfaced. The car speeded up suburbanization, facilitating the pursuit of leisure activities, including the increasingly popular game of golf, in new clubs such as the Singapore Island Country Club, the Seletar Flying Club and the Turf Club at Bukit Timah. Public transport also received a boost with the advent of the trackless trolleybus, and the extension of its service to new suburban areas. In 1930, Singapore was said to have the largest trolleybus system in the world. Privately owned 'mosquito' buses—large motor car chassis built up as eight-seater minibuses—were a serious competitor.

As a port city, Singapore became more exposed to new consumer products and Western popular culture, sports and media. American and British films were popular, and rich and poor alike patronized the new picture houses. The first commercial wireless station was established in 1915, but wireless sets did not come into common usage until the British Malayan Broadcasting Corporation was set up in 1936. Singapore Cold Storage started to manufacture ice cream, while Malayan Breweries launched locally made beer.

It was called 'Malaya's Premier Picture Palace'. When Capitol Cinema opened on 22 May 1930 the public was in awe of the lavish interior, a view echoed by a reporter of The Straits Times *who commented that 'the stage is almost too elaborate for a mere cinema'.*

Interior of barracks, mid-1930s. Shifting strategic alliances in Asia after World War I led Britain to develop a naval base in Singapore and build up the island's seaward defences. Post World War II, the British maintained their military presence until total withdrawal in October 1971.

Many Europeans and wealthy Asians lived comfortably in spacious bungalows in shady suburbs, tended to by a retinue of servants. The small but growing English-educated middle class was settling in more modest bungalows in suburbs like Katong and Siglap. Opium dens were fast disappearing with controls on opium smoking. In 1927, the importation of girls for prostitution was stopped, and, three years later, brothels were closed, forcing prostitution to go underground. But, the city was still famous for its less savoury aspects. Willis' mid-1930s *Singapore Guide* felt it necessary to caution visitors, 'A great amount of nonsense has been written about Singapore, and it will help visitors to an early appreciation of the place, if we state here explicitly that it is not the wicked place which many people have said it is.'

While some benefits, in the form of health care and employment opportunities, filtered down to the masses, the vast majority lived in buildings condemned as 'unfit for human habitation'. The problem did not go unnoticed. In 1918, the government appointed a Housing Commission to investigate 'housing difficulties'. According to the Commission, 'Asian ignorance and apathy' were largely responsible for the state of affairs. Still, improvements needed to be planned. Discussions centred on the degree to which the colonial and municipal governments were responsible for counteracting 'Asiatic insanitary standards', and whether such efforts would be of any avail. The outcome of the report was the creation of the Singapore Improvement Trust (SIT) in 1927. But with limited powers, vague goals, insufficient funds and weak political will, it barely scratched the surface before war reached the shores of Singapore, and Japanese soldiers marched across the Causeway.

The photographs here are from a red leather album which belonged to Lee Poh Neo, the daughter of Mr and Mrs Lee Choon Guan of Mandalay Villa. They were taken to record the visit of Edward, Prince of Wales and later Duke of Windsor, who was on a tour of the Far East. Among his official duties during the two-day visit were the unveiling of the Cenotaph, which was built to commemorate those who lost their lives in World War I, and the opening of the Malaya Borneo Exhibition (1).

The photographs form a unique portrait of the city at a particular moment in time, and include some of the buildings with which the Lee family had a special connection. The Chinese Commercial Bank (3) was started by the Amoy-born pioneer of Singapore industry Lim Peng Siang as well as other members of the Hokkien business community. The first chairman was Lee Choon Guan. In 1932, the bank merged with the Ho Hong Bank and the Oversea-Chinese Bank to form the Oversea-Chinese Banking Corporation.

Lim Nee Soon Building (5) was built circa 1920 to the design of Seah & Le Cain Civil Engineers, Architects & Surveyors at the corner of Robinson Road and McCallum Street. Mr Lim, a pioneer rubber planter, founded his own business in 1911. His son, Lim Chong Pang, married Lee Poh Neo in 1924.

The Chartered Bank Building (6) at Raffles Place was completed in 1915, and demolished in 1952. Its former premises in Battery Road (4) had several tenants by the 1920s, including the Bank of Taiwan. It was demolished to make way for the Bank of China Building, built in 1953–4. Amber Mansions (7) was one of the earliest apartment buildings in the city, surviving until the 1980s when it was demolished to build Dhoby Ghaut MRT Station. Raffles Chambers (8) became home of Robinson & Co. department store in 1941, but was destroyed in an infamous fire in 1972 which also killed nine people.

1 *The Prince of Wales attends the Malaya Borneo Exhibition organized in Singapore, April 1922. This and all views of the buildings decorated for the event are from an album inscribed 'Lee Poh Neo, Mandalay Villa, Katong, Souvenirs of the Visit of HRH The Prince of Wales and the Malaya Borneo Exhibition, March–April 1922'.*
2 *Empress Place*
3 *The Chinese Commercial Bank Ltd, 64 Chulia Street*
4 *Among the tenants of the former premises of the Chartered Bank Building in Battery Road was the Bank of Taiwan*
5 *Lim Nee Soon Building*
6 *Chartered Bank Building, Raffles Place*
7 *Lower end of Orchard Road showing Amber Mansions*
8 *Raffles Chambers in Raffles Place*
9 *Hotel de l'Europe*

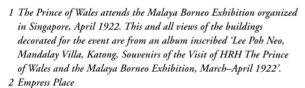

4

6

7

8

5

9

During the 1920s, tremendous advances in aviation were made. Work on Singapore's first purpose-built airport, an air base at Seletar, commenced in 1927. Strides were also made in organizing the routing of planes for carrying air mail, but passenger traffic was still a secondary consideration. In 1930, the Straits Settlements government allowed the landing of commercial aircraft at Seletar Air Base, an arrangement that continued until the official opening of Kallang Airport (3) on 12 June 1937. It had taken six years to turn the 'evil-smelling tidal swamp' near town into a modern airport. Reclamation involved the resettlement of several kampongs and the moving of nearly 6 million cubic metres of earth. The terminal, which still stands, is an early example of the Modern International Style transplanted to the tropics.

1 The novelty of a seaplane attracts youthful attention, 1930s
2 Inscribed 'Chanteloup, L. N. S. [at centre] and S. K. T. Singapore 9 May 1924. 5.30 p.m.'. The initials 'L. N. S.' are Lim Nee Soon's.
3 Crowds at Kallang after the official opening on 12 June 1937
4 The control tower, Kallang Airport, 1939
5 Terminal under construction, mid-1930s
6 Airport in use, 1939

1

2

3

4

5

6

One of the most profoundly experienced changes during this period was the increase in people's mobility. The car changed how cities were planned, speeded up suburbanization and gave unprecedented mobility to women.

Registered motor vehicles increased from 842 in 1915, to 9,477 in 1931 to 17,514 in 1941. There was also an increase in the number of passengers availing themselves of public transport after the Singapore Traction Company was formed in 1925 to run trackless trolleybuses. Robert Foran recorded that traffic in the 1930s was 'no less astonishing for its quantity and variety than that of the masses of craft in the roadstead or on the congested river. Everyone appears to own a car … The tally of the Malay- and Chinese-operated taxis and buses must run into the four figures or more. Motor lorries, private and public cars and buses, horse or bullock drawn carts, man hauled rickshaws [sic], and a vast multitude of bicycles flood the streets.'

1 *A motorized hearse at the funeral of Oei Tiong Ham, 1924*
2 *New fire engines proudly displayed at the Hill Street Fire Station*
3 *Trolleybus accident, late 1920s*
4 *Traffic police, 1930s*
5–6 *Accidents on the roads, 1920s*
7–8 *Posing with car, early 1930s*

1

3

4

5

6

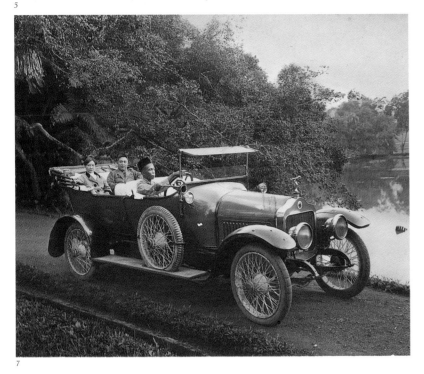

7

8

1

2

3

4

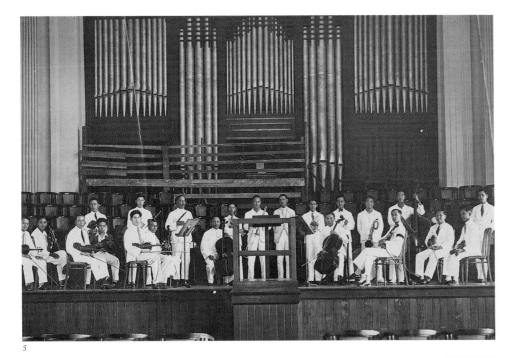

5

6

7

8

9

A new pipe organ at Victoria Memorial Hall (5) and cabarets in amusement parks (7 and 9) were among the new forms of entertainment, but it was the cinema that thrived. During the 1920s, movies came into their own. Cinema became a great social leveller, eroding the mystique surrounding the colonial elite. By the mid-1930s, there were 10 cinemas, of which the Capitol (1) was the largest and newest. It opened in 1930, and was followed by the Alhambra (3), Marlborough, Pavilion, Roxy, Wembly, Tivoli (4), Empire, Jubilee and Gaiety.

Cathay Building and Cinema (8) opened on 3 October 1939 with a showing of Alexander Korda's *The Four Feathers*. The 1,300-seat cinema was a harbinger of things to come. Air-conditioned and fitted out with armchairs, it had a crush hall with black marble pillars, green tiled floors and gold ceilings. The 16-storey Cathay Building was Singapore's first skyscraper, twice as high as the tallest structure then, the Union Building, and made of reinforced concrete. Designed by Frank Brewer, the 32 luxury flats on offer came with hot and cold water, refrigerators and the use of a squash court. The apartments were completed in August 1941. But with the war imminent, the building was leased to the government, and housed the Department of Broadcasting.

1 *Interior of Capitol Cinema, 1930*
2 *Jubilee Theatre, c. 1938*
3 *The Alhambra, c. 1938*
4 *The Tivoli screened only Chinese movies*
5 *Classical music at Victoria Memorial Hall, c. 1938*
6 *Chinese string orchestra, 1930s*
7 *New World Cabaret, late 1930s*
8 *Cathay Cinema, c. 1940*
9 *The crowds at Great World, 1930s*

For the affluent of all races and the small but growing Asian middle class, there was more time for leisure and sports, while the car now permitted travel further afield. Sports clubs were, however, still organized mainly along racial lines. While the Changi Sailing Club (1) and the newly rebuilt Singapore Swimming Club (2) were patronized by Europeans, the Singapore Chinese Swimming Club (7) was producing its own champion teams.

One common ground for all races, and all classes, was the racetrack. The Turf Club moved into its new home (3) on 15 April 1933. The track, a three-storey grandstand and a trio of car parks with room for a thousand vehicles, rose out of a former rubber plantation. Some 100 hectares were acquired at 90 cents a square metre from the Bukit Timah Rubber Estate. Work began with the clearance of 30,000 trees, the moving of hillocks and the filling in of valleys to create what the press hailed as 'undoubtedly one of the finest racecourses in the East'.

Golf was also gaining popularity. The Singapore Golf Club was a European enclave, but in 1924 the Racecourse Golf Club (so named because of its location at the racecourse) opened its door to all ethnic groups. When the Turf Club moved to Bukit Timah, the Racecourse Golf Club secured land near Pierce Reservoir for an 18-hole course which it called the Island Club. It was officially opened in 1932 by Governor Sir Cecil Clementi Smith, who remarked that the club deserved 'the support of all Singapore because it provides the means of fraternization on the field of sport between all races and communities'.

1 Changi Sailing Club, 1930s
2 Singapore Swimming Club, new clubhouse completed in 1936
3 Singapore Turf Club, completed in 1933
4 Women begin to compete in swimming, 1930s
5 Pole vaulting, 1930s
6 Tennis, 1920s
7 Members of the Singapore Chinese Swimming Club, 1930s
8 Group photo of martial arts team of Foong Shoon Wei Kuan, c. 1940

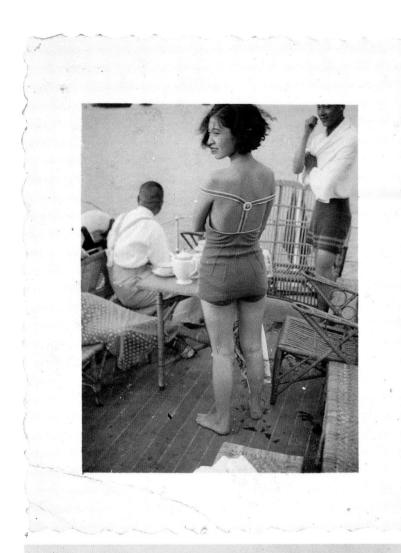

6

5

7

8

Medical care began to improve generally with the opening of new hospitals and the introduction of public health schemes, such as anti-malarial work, sewage disposal and the proper maintenance of the water supply.

During the 1920s, the government embarked on an ambitious hospital-building programme: the new General Hospital (6) and the Trafalgar Home for Lepers were both built in 1926, Woodbridge Mental Hospital in 1927, Kandang Kerbau Maternity Hospital in 1928 and Alexandra and Changi Hospitals in 1935. These were staffed largely by graduates of the King Edward VII College of Medicine, which moved into its new premises (1 and 5) in 1927.

Private hospitals carried on playing an important role, especially in administering to the poor and needy. In particular, Tan Tock Seng continued to provide free medical services to the poor. One of the newer hospitals, Kwong Wai Shui Free Hospital (4), was opened by a Cantonese clan in 1910 to treat patients suffering from chronic diseases.

St Andrew's Mission Hospital started in 1913, with the avowed intention of giving Asian women, especially those who were poor, the option of being seen by a doctor of their own sex. In 1923, St Andrew's settled into its own purpose built 60-bed hospital at Erskine Road in Chinatown. It also pioneered training for nurses and midwives to tackle the high infant mortality rate, which was due both to unskilled midwifery and poor conditions such as poverty, bad housing, overcrowding, unsanitary surroundings, the lack of knowledge on the part of mothers and the improper feeding of infants. The hospital also took in blind children, and opened an eye clinic as well as a clinic for venereal diseases.

In 1927, Singapore's first Public Health Nurse, a Miss Simpson, urged that a government travelling dispensary be set up to serve the rural areas where diseases were common. This was launched in 1930, with weekly sessions at the Bukit Timah Outpatient Dispensary. New immigrants passed through St John's Island (2 and 3), where they were screened for diseases and quarantined if necessary.

1 Biochemistry laboratory, King Edward VII College of Medicine, c. 1928
2–3 Health screening of new immigrants on St John's Island, c. 1920
4 The Board of Kwong Wai Shui Free Hospital poses for a photograph outside the hospital gates, January 1926
5 The opening of King Edward VII College of Medicine Building, 1927
6 General Hospital ward with Christmas decorations, 1930s

5

6

More children were spending an increasing amount of time in the classroom (2, 3, and 4) as the demand for education grew concurrently with economic expansion and employment opportunities. The authorities subsidized four years of primary schooling for Malay children, gave substantial subsidies to government and government-aided English-medium schools and small grants to certain Chinese and Tamil schools. By 1939, there were 72,000 children at school, of whom 38,000 studied in Chinese schools, 27,000 in English schools, 6,000 in Malay schools and 1,000 in Tamil schools. Yet, many children, especially girls, still did not attend school.

Victoria School, a second government English-medium secondary school, opened in 1931. C. M. Turnbull describes its impact in *A History of Singapore 1819–1975*, 'This created a common bond between the talented and ambitious elite of different racial groups, but often cut them off from their cultural roots and separated them from the mass of their own community. This danger was beginning to be appreciated in the 1930s, and the McLean Commission advocated teaching vernacular as second languages in English-medium schools. Nothing came of this before World War II, and the education system remained racially and socially divisive. It offered a promising career for the English-educated minority but condemned the mass of the vernacular educated to unskilled work.' The English educated had little difficulty in finding white collar jobs until the onset of the Great Depression, when the shock of unemployment invited criticism that English education was too bookish and should perhaps have a more practical bent.

Raffles College (6) was conceived as a memorial to celebrate Singapore's centenary, but it was 10 years from the announcement in 1918 to the admission of 43 students in June 1928. The land along Bukit Timah Road was donated by the Straits Settlements government, the buildings—the result of an international architectural competition—were designed by Cyril A. Farey and Graham R. Dawbarn and the endowment fund supported by prominent businessmen including Sir Manasseh Meyer, Oei Tiong Ham, Tan Soo Guan and Eu Tong Sen.

1 High school students, 1920s
2 Lim Lam San (see pages 190 and 223) and his students, Telok Kurau English School, 1920s
3–4 In the classroom, 1920s
5 Students of the Straits Commercial College, a private school in Geylang, mark the Silver Jubilee of King George V, 1935
6 Inscribed 'The Historical and Economics Societies Combined Fancy Dress Social at the Oei Tiong Ham Hall, Raffles College, 25 October 1941'
7–8 Class portraits were an important momento of school days

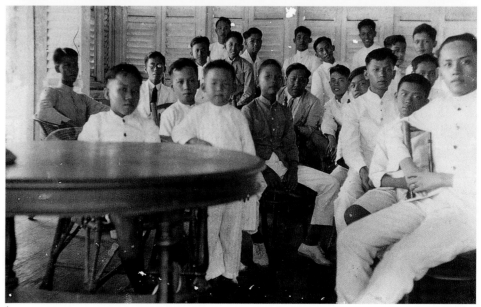

5

The Historical & Economics Societies Combined Fancy Dress Social, at the Oei Tiong Ham Hall, Raffles College, October 25th, 1941.

6

7

8

崇福女校改組後第一屆初級高級畢業生及全體教職員撮影 克章

The Singaporean Chinese contributed handsomely to establishing schools in both Singapore and China. Most of the schools were financially supported by clan associations. Teachers and text books were imported from China, orientating youth to the Chinese motherland, whether from a Communist or from a Kuomintang perspective. Yet for Chinese graduates, there was no avenue to the civil service or to the non-Chinese commercial world. The vast majority of Chinese-educated children received only primary schooling. An important milestone was the opening of the Chinese High School on 21 March 1919—the first middle school in the region teaching boys in Mandarin, *hua yu*, up to pre-university level.

1 *Chong Hock Girls' School, 1920s*
2 *Graduating class, Nanyang Girls' School, 1920s*
3 *Students and staff of Tao Nan School, 1920s*
4 *Board of Directors of Qi Fa, a well-known Hakka school, 1932*
5 *Yoke Eng High School, set up by the Hainanese clan associations, had its humble beginnings in Prinsep Street*
6 *Yeung Ching School was started by the Cantonese in 1905 in what was the ancestral home of Chia Ann Siang, on Ann Siang Hill*

3

新嘉坡茶陽會館暨啟發學校同人歡迎鄒敬初先生攝影紀念 二十二年二月

4

5

6

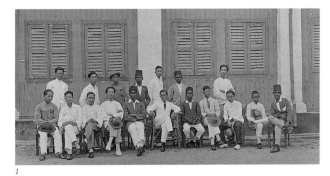

1

For the children of the middle class, there were now ample ways of enjoying oneself outside the classroom. Music, dance, scouts, school excursions and sports offered opportunities for personal development and self-expression. School sports days (7–9) usually drew cheering crowds. Netball and hockey were relatively new games. The Girls' Sports Club established by and for Eurasian women in 1930 started a hockey team (11) that quickly established itself as a leading team.

Most of the photographs here are from an album compiled by Lim Lam San, who taught at Telok Kurau English School in the 1920s. There his pupils included the young Lee Kuan Yew. An enthusiastic photographer, Lim frequently brought his camera along to record school events and outings.

1 Inscribed 'Group photo of Standard VI, 1926'
2 Young musicians, Telok Kurau English School, 1920s
3 Dancing, girls' school style
4 Amateur Badminton Association, 2 October 1927
5 Gan Eng Seng School scouts with scoutmaster, Mr Tara Singh, c. 1926
6 Gan Eng Seng School visit to Siong Lim Temple, late 1920s
7 School sports day, the three-legged race
8 Visitors at the sports
9 Interclass drill competition
10 Telok Kurau English School, 1928
11 Eurasian girls' hockey team, 1930s

4

2

5

3

6

7

8

9

10

11

Municipal Building, Singapore

The final stage in the evolution of the historical civic centre took place in the 1920s and 1930s, when the colonial government embarked on an ambitious building programme. The Municipal Building (3) was constructed in 1926–9 to the design of Municipal Architect F. D. Meadows, who exploited the prestigious setting by designing a dramatic facade featuring 18 colossal Corinthian columns. The building housed the Municipal Council chambers and other offices.

The Supreme Court (5) was designed by Municipal Architect F. Dorrington Ward, and constructed on the site of the Hotel de l'Europe which closed in 1932. Many of the architectural components so essential to this Classical-Revival style were manufactured in the studio of Rudolpho Nolli at 47 Scotts Road (4 and 8–10). Nolli (1888–1963) was born in Milan, and came to the Far East with a group of Italian artists, painters and sculptors commissioned by the Siamese government to decorate the King's new Throne Hall. He moved to Singapore in 1921.

Other additions to the civic district include the Cenotaph (1) and the Tan Kim Seng Fountain (2), which was moved to this seafront location from Fullerton Square.

1 *The Cenotaph was unveiled by the visiting Prince of Wales, 1922*
2 *Tan Kim Seng Fountain was moved to the Esplanade, mid-1920s*
3 *Municipal Building (City Hall) shortly after completion in 1929*
4 *Nolli's workmen pose in an inverted Ionic capital*
5 *The last of Singapore's colonial classical buildings, dramatically lit*
6 *Component of the 14-ton Allegory of Justice photographed in Nolli's studio before installation in the Supreme Court pediment*
7 *The view from the top of Supreme Court, 1939*
8 *Premises of R. Nolli & Co. Inscribed 'For Hongkong Shanghai Bank, Battery Road, Singapore, 1923'*
9 *Awaiting installation, the Coat of Arms for Fullerton Building*
10 *Nolli's premises at 47 Scotts Road*

5

7

8

9

6

10

1

2

3

4

5

6

7

8

The Fullerton Building, housing a new General Post Office, was completed in 1928 to the design of Keyes and Dowdeswell, a Shanghai-based firm of architects who came to Singapore after winning the open architectural competition for the project. The building was made of steel and reinforced concrete (1–3). A final touch to the exterior was the official crest (4), which was made in the workshop of Rodolpho Nolli (see previous pages). The General Post Office occupied the lower floors with sorting rooms, offices and a spacious postal hall (6). The upper floors were used by the now-defunct Singapore Club, which was established in 1862. From 1876, it was located in the Chamber of Commerce and Singapore Exchange Building which was demolished to make way for the Fullerton Building. The Club's luxurious facilities included a billiard room (7), a bar and lounge (8) and sleeping accommodation.

1–3 *Fullerton Building photographed at various stages of construction, mid-1920s*
4 *The main entrance*
5 *The entrance hall*
6 *The postal hall*
7 *The billiard room of the Singapore Club on the building's upper floors*
8 *The Club's bar and lounge*

Along Collyer Quay several new buildings appeared, which presented a Bund-like skyline to ships passing through the Straits of Singapore. The larger scale and longer spans of the Maritime Building (2), the Ocean Building (3) and the Hongkong and Shanghai Bank (4) were made possible by new construction techniques. The application of classical elements and the stone-like claddings gave the facades a solid and enduring appearance that echoed the confidence of Empire. Another change was the removal of the old Johnston Pier and the transfer of ferry activities to the new Clifford Pier (1).

1 Improved sea links: Clifford Pier, completed in 1931
2 Union Building at Collyer Quay after completion in 1924
3 The new Ocean Building, built in 1921-3
4 The new Hongkong and Shanghai Bank, completed in 1925
5 Panorama of Raffles Place, 1920s. The square has been converted to a car park overlooked by several new buildings.

3

4

1

3

2

Prosperity also encouraged some new building in Chinatown. One new landmark was the China Building (1), completed in 1932 on Chulia Street and designed by Major Keys of the Shanghai-based firm Keys and Dodswell. It was suitably adorned with Chinese architectural embellishments, including an upturned roof, to house the newly formed Oversea-Chinese Banking Corporation, which was an amalgamation of three Chinese banks: the Chinese Commercial Bank, Ho Hong Bank and the Oversea-Chinese Bank.

These three smaller banks, all founded by Chinese merchants between 1910 and 1920, were badly bruised by the economic turmoil of the Great Depression of 1929–33, which brought the rubber estates, plantations and mines of Malaya to the very edge of ruin. Amalgamation was seen as a chance to gain strength. The Bank opened for business on 2 January 1933, one of the largest and strongest local banks in the Straits Settlements. In 1972, the building was demolished.

The new Chinese Protectorate (2), Tanjong Pagar Police Station (5) and Kwangtung Provincial Bank (4) were all built during the 1930s. The new premises of Yee Shing Co. Ltd (9) were next to offices of the Lee Rubber Company.

4

1 China Building, completed 1932, in an early 1950s photograph
2 The new Chinese Protectorate Building, after rebuilding, c. 1923
3 Premises of Fook On emporium at South Bridge Road
4 Inscribed 'Kwangtung Provincial Bank'
5 Tanjong Pagar Police Station, photographed in late 1930s
6 Wah Sun Tobacco
7 Chinese medicine hall, Da De Shang Yao
8 Chinese Products Emporium, new location at No. 24 South Bridge Road
9 Yee Shing Co. Ltd, with premises of Lee Rubber on the right

5

6

7

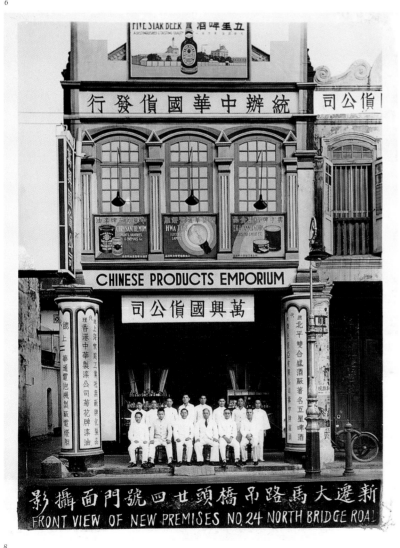

8

9

Eu Villa (1) was, in many ways, the quintessential early 19th-century Singapore mansion, a flamboyant and eclectic mixture of architectural elements in the style favoured by wealthy Straits Chinese. It was completed in the mid-1910s and inhabited by the Eu family until 1973, when it was sold to a property developer who demolished it in the early 1980s.

The Mount Sophia premises overlooked Dhoby Ghaut, and was purchased in 1912 by Eu Tong Sen (1877–1940), the son of Eu Kong, a prominent tin miner. The young Eu was sent to China for his education but returned in 1891 when his father died. He expanded his father's business, founded Eu Yan Sang, a company dealing in Chinese medicine, and, by the time he was 30 was one of the richest men in the region.

Eu pulled down the existing house and employed the firm of Swan & Maclaren to design a new home. If the architecture followed established tradition, the structure was particularly modern: the house was constructed partially in reinforced concrete, and had large column-free areas made possible by steel joists and reinforced concrete floors.

The five-storey building was one of the largest residences on the island. It included a basement, which accommodated the kitchen, a wine cellar and 10 bedrooms. The main living rooms were in the front of the house, offering a magnificent view of the harbour and the town. No expense was spared in the furnishing, and the interior was decorated with furniture, art and statues bought from well-known firms in Paris and London.

1 Eu Tong Sen's mansion, Mount Sophia, photographed c. 1920
2 Amah and garden statuary, c. 1920
3 The living room with furniture ordered from Paris and London
4 One of the villa's 10 bedrooms
5 A bathroom with Art Nouveau details
6–10 Other examples of bungalow styles, 1920s

6

8

9

7

10

Amongst the suburban neighbourhoods settled by affluent Chinese were Blair Road (1) and Emerald Hill Road (2), where terraced houses were built between 1900 and 1930. The style of mixing Chinese and Western elements has been variously referred to as Coarsened Classical, Chinese Baroque, Straits Chinese and Chinese Eclectic. Emerald Hill Road was formed in 1901; nearly two-thirds of the houses were erected between 1900 and 1918, the remaining one-third around 1925.

Frank Brewer employed a distinctive style inspired by the Arts and Crafts movement in the houses he designed during his 30 years in Singapore. Signature elements evident in a Ridout Road house (3) are the exposed bricks and textured plasterwork.

The 1930s saw the arrival of the Modern International Style in projects as diverse as the Singapore Improvement Trust's (SIT) artisans' flats (5) and the house of millionaires Aw Boon Haw and Aw Boon Par designed by Ho Kwong Yew (4). All of the buildings erected by the SIT during the 1930s bore the stamp of the Modern Movement in their flat roofs, curved balconies, horizontal ribbon windows and white cubist look.

1 *Residential terraces at Blair Road, 1920s*
2 *No. 45, Emerald Hill Road terrace house, constructed 1903, photographed mid-1920s*
3 *House of L.W. Geddes, Ridout Road, designed by Frank Brewer, 1934,*
4 *Modern International Style house, Pasir Panjang, late 1930s*
5 *SIT artisans' houses at Balestier, constructed 1932–40*

1

2

3

4

5

1

2

3

The Singapore River continued to play a crucial role in the island's economy and was as jammed as ever with *tongkang* and other small craft. But by the 1930s, lorries had largely replaced bullock carts as the main means of transporting goods. The old shophouses along south Boat Quay (left), were already showing signs of age, appearing here very much worn out and run down. There was surprisingly little rebuilding along the river in the two decades preceding World War II. One exception was the new Central Police Station at Hill Street (3), built in conjunction with the modernization of the police force.

LEFT *Congested south Boat Quay was a popular postcard view*
1 *Elgin Bridge was rebuilt in 1926*
2 *This view towards the mouth of the river is inscribed 'Sampans at Singapore'*
3 *Hill Street Police Station under construction, c. 1933*

1

3

4

The increased urbanization of the Municipality is illustrated in these mainly postcard views from the 1920s and 1930s. Orchard Road (4) was lined with shop-houses. Trolleybuses

2

shared main thoroughfares, such as High Street (3) and North Bridge Road (6), with rickshaws, cars, bicycles and the occasional bullock cart. Side streets were mainly the preserve of the rickshaw puller and pedestrian. Old shophouses were giving way to larger buildings, including several apartment blocks. Flooding could be a problem during the monsoon season (9–12), seriously affecting the arterial roads.

1 Rickshaw puller, open drains and shophouses on Prinsep Street, 1920s
2 Inscribed 'Killiney Road, 1929', Chia Keng Thye, photographer
3 High Street with tram, 1920s postcard
4 Orchard Road, looking south, view taken from railway bridge
5 Malay Street
6 Meyer Flats, the first multi-storey apartment building, North Bridge Road
7 New buildings along Beach Road
8 Hylam Street
9 Flooding on Orchard Road, outside Cold Storage, mid–1920s
10 More Orchard Road flooding, in front of Amber Mansions
11 Waterlogged streets near Ellenborough Market
12 The water rises outside Telok Ayer Market

5

6

9

7

10

11

8

12

1

3

The scenes here offer a different perspective of street life which bears little resemblance to typical picture-postcard views. They are from an album of amateur photographs which seem to have been taken during a burst of photographic activity around 1938, and were donated to the National Archives of Singapore by the Goh family. The photographs were taken by a family member whose name has not, unfortunately, been recorded. The images are surprisingly modern and strongly documentary, as if the photographer deliberately focused his camera on scenes which he knew would one day disappear. The Holloway Lane context of the shophouses on the facing page is fixed by St Joseph's Church at Victoria Street. Selections from the Goh family albums appear elsewhere in this chapter.

FACING PAGE *Holloway Lane, c. 1938*
1 Malay women, c. 1938
2 Lantern shop, South Bridge Road, c. 1938
3 Chinese women, c. 1938
4 Coolies loading coal, Keppel Harbour, c. 1938

2

4

Chinese Street, Singapore

1

2

3

4

5

6

7

8

9

10

There were few uncrowded rooms in the slums of Chinatown. Thousands jammed into coolie lodgings, most of which had neither running water nor toilets. Many of the older buildings were still back-to-back, so that lighting and ventilation were inadequate. Cage-like cubicles and single bunks served as rooms, each separated from the next by tea boxes and canvas sacks. All tenants shared common kitchens, bathrooms and latrines. Because housing was so scarce, and the demand so high, landlords could charge exorbitant rents. The deplorable living conditions were investigated as early as 1907 in Dr W. J. Simpson's *Report on the Sanitary Conditions of Singapore*, and again in 1918 in the Report of the Housing Commission. But, conditions continued to deteriorate. In 1927, the Singapore Improvement Trust (SIT) was formed. Its objectives were framed in the broadest terms: 'to provide for the Improvement of the Town and Island of Singapore.' Housing was obviously a critical issue. A sum of $10 million, designated for slum clearance by the government in 1926, was allocated for its use.

Initially the SIT had no power to build, but was obliged to provide accommodation for people displaced by slum clearance. A series of enactments widened its powers, and, from 1936 until the fall of Singapore, it completed 2,049 houses and 54 shops, including low-rise apartment blocks in Chinatown and the first phase of a new town in Tiong Bahru. Yet it had barely made an impact on the problem. The SIT building in Smith Street (10) was used by the Japanese Secret Police during World War II. It was demolished in 1975.

1 Classic Chinatown view, 1920s
2 New Bridge Road, c. 1930
3 Inscribed 'Rickshaw coolie quarters', postcard, 1930s
4 Telok Ayer Street, 1920s
5 Junction of Smith Street and Trengganu Street, 1920s
6 South BridgeRoad, c. 1930
7–9 Chinatown streets, 1930s
10 SIT flats in Smith Street, built in 1938

Amongst the urban landmarks to be given a refurbishment during these years was Sri Mariamman Temple. When extensive renovations were carried out in the 1930s, the *gopuram*, or tower (6), was rebuilt. Sri Perumal Temple (2) dates back to the mid-1850s, although the structure shown here was a later reconstruction. The Tank Road Temple (4) was started by the Chettiars, a caste of South Indians, mainly traders, bankers and moneylenders from near Madras. Great wealth was poured into the temple when it was built in the later part of the 19th century. Included in its treasures were two silver chariots (5) paraded through the streets on festivals such as Thaipusam.

Photographs of Thaipusam (1, 3, 4 and 5) became popular during the 1920s and 1930s. This festival is celebrated annually, usually in February, when Hindu devotees traditionally gather to prepare for their act of devotion and thanksgiving. Only men, however, carry the *kavadi*. Roland Braddell writing in 1934, in *The Lights of Singapore*, described Thaipusam as 'the occasion when Subramanian, the particular god of Chettiars, revealed himself to his devotees riding on a peacock … [and] is taken round the town in solemn procession in the large silver car, drawn by two sacred white buffaloes, and a great reception is held at the temple to which all are welcome …'

1 *Thaipusam chariot, 1930s*
2 *Sri Perumal Temple, Serangoon Road*
3 *Thaipusam penitent, Thaipusam 1930s*
4 *Tank Road Temple during Thaipusam*
5 *Inscribed 'The Silver Car being drawn through the Streets'*
6 *Sri Mariamman Temple, c. 1938*

1

2

3

4

5

1

The original Sultan Mosque was constructed in 1824–6. In its centenary year, the trustees approved the erection of a new building on the site. The construction took four years to complete, and was undertaken in phases so that worship would never be disrupted. Funds were generously contributed from Muslims of all communities. The design, by Denis Santry of Swan & Maclaren, employed the Islamic Saracenic style which was a synthesis of historic forms from the diverse heritages of India and Islam combined with British standards of utility and modernity. In front of the mosque and under the trolleybus wires (2) is a 'mosquito' bus, a common sight on the roads.

1 *Malay procession, 1937*
2 AND RIGHT *Two views of Sultan Mosque and Kampong Glam environs*

2

For the poor and illiterate there were many ways to make a living on the streets—from grinding coffee (1) and selling drinks (2) to hawking vegetables (4) and telling fortunes (9). Itinerant hawkers (7) were a common sight throughout the town, their poles and cooking pots eagerly lowered to cater to the appetites of the hungry. Age and sex were no barrier, and young girls could be seen scavenging for rags (6), this image embellishing a Singapore postcard sold during the 1930s.

And then there were the rickshaw pullers (following pages). From its introduction in 1880 until their disappearance on the eve of World War II, rickshaws offered cheap and efficient transportation for ordinary people whose only alternative was to walk. By the turn of the century, it was virtually impossible to take a photograph of any street without the proverbial rickshaw and its puller somewhere in the background. For the pullers it was a grim life. Many took up the work upon arrival from China and viewed it enthusiastically only to be condemned to a life of poverty and debt. Few pullers ever owned their vehicles. And living conditions in coolie rickshaw quarters were deplorable.

By 1924, the number of active rickshaw pullers on the road was estimated at 28,800. But their days were numbered. Although it remained a convenient mode of transport patronized by people from all walks of life, it had lost some of its traditional customers to the fleets of trolleybuses, running on regular schedules, and motor vehicles including the 'mosquito' buses. Officials now viewed rickshaws as a slow and hazardous mode of conveyance, arguing that they impeded the traffic flow. In 1928, the number of rickshaw licences issued was lowered and the vehicles were banned from some parts of the city. A major strike by pullers in 1938 ended in failure. Many returned to China before the outbreak of war. Others made the transition to the bicycle-driven trishaw.

1 Roasting coffee beans
2 Selling drinks
3 A vending cart
4 Vegetables in the streets
5 Stacking firewood imported from Indonesia, early 1930s
6 Rag gatherers
7 Street hawker
8 Malay stall
9 Fortune telling

FOLLOWING PAGES Jinrickshaw puller at the corner of North Bridge and Rochor Roads, mid-1930s

4

5

6

7

8

9

1

Several Malay areas changed fundamentally under pressures of increased urbanization, population growth and infrastructure projects. In Kampong Glam, the steep rise in land values, expansion of commercial activities and construction of shophouses largely erased the remaining residential quality of the area. Geylang Serai (facing page), where land was still cheap, was transformed from a rural community to a suburb. Much of the land had been the Alsagoff family's former Perseverance Estate, which produced lemon grass oil from the *serai* and citronella plants until the 1890s. Along the *lorong*, or lanes, there was much construction activity.

Other families settled further east in Kampong Melayu in Jalan Eunos. The community was specially created on a 240-hectare site reserved by the Legislative Council to preserve the kampong way of life. It was here that Malays from Kallang Basin were resettled to make way for Kallang Airport. Several other official Malay villages were set up around the island.

FACING PAGE **Geylang Road, postcard view, early 1920s**
1 *Malay hawkers, 1930s*
2 *Inscribed 'Malay* kolek *racing at Bedoh. Preparing for the Start'*

2

GELANG ROAD
SINGAPORE

1

2

3

4

8

9

6

7

After World War I, Katong developed from a weekend retreat into a permanent residential suburb. The land had become available for residential building after the fragmentation of the large coconut plantations. Cars and new roads now linked suburb and city. Motorized transport made living further from town more attractive and practical, while the trolleybus made the area accessible to the middle class.

By the 1930s, Katong was a mixture of large bungalows, kampongs and middle-class housing, including the shophouses and residential terraces of Joo Chiat and Koon Seng Roads. Swimming near Katong Pier (8 and 9) was a popular pastime.

The photographs of Joo Chiat (1–4) are from an album by Lim Lam San (1902–90). Lim, then a teacher at Telok Kurau English School, was an avid amateur photographer during the 1920s and 1930s, who concentrated on capturing scenes of everyday life, such as friends eating curry puffs and the interior of his home (2 and 4). Most of the photographs are dated and captioned, and were printed from glass plates in the darkroom of his Joo Chiat home. One, of Joo Chiat Road (3), shows just how rural the area still was in 1919.

1 'Song Cheng, Quek Seng Yong, Seng Ho and Curry Puff Vendor at Joo Chiat Place' from the album Sunny Memories kept by Lim Lam San
2 Bedroom scene, dated 17 April 1934
3 Inscribed 'Joo Chiat Road, 1919'
4 Inscribed 'The Sitting Room at 48 Joo Chiat Place, 1926'
5–7 Tanjong Katong, postcard views, 1920s
8 Katong Pier, built in 1915, was destroyed by the British at the beginning of the war
9 Swimming by the Pier, 1930s

1

2

3

4

5

6

9

7

8

Mandalay Villa was one of the great houses of prewar Singapore. The large airy structure was built in 1902 as a weekend retreat by millionaire Lee Cheng Yan. In 1900, Lee Cheng Yan's widowed son, Lee Choon Guan, married Tan Teck Neo, the third daughter of the equally prominent businessman Tan Keong Saik. Several years later, the couple made Mandalay Villa, at 29 Amber Road, their home.

Mrs Lee (1877–1978) grew up in the cloistered and privileged world of the wealthy Straits Chinese. She was tutored in English at home, but after her marriage emerged as one of the leading figures of Singapore society. In 1915, she founded the Chinese Women's Association and, three years later, was honoured as a Member of the Order of the British Empire (MBE) for her charitable work as well as for her contribution to the British Red Cross. She was presented at the Court of St James, and attended a royal garden party at Buckingham Palace. She was very fond of dancing and well known for her diamonds (3).

The couple had two children, a son, Pang Soo, and a daughter, Poh Neo. In 1924, Poh Neo married Lim Chong Pang, son of millionaire rubber pioneer Lim Nee Soon (9) (see pages 98–9). As was common then, the couple lived in the wife's home. The same year saw the death of Lee Choon Guan (8).

The sea pavilion (1) had two bedrooms gilded by Italian artists, one used by Mrs Lee and the other by her daughter and son-in-law. It was demolished by the British forces before the war in anticipation of a Japanese invasion from the sea. After the war, as the family grew larger, many of the rooms in the main house were partitioned into smaller ones and some of the hallways were even converted into bedrooms.

Mrs Lee continued to live in Mandalay Villa until her death at the age of 101. Not long after, the house was sold by the family. It was torn down in 1983.

---

1 The sea pavilion at Mandalay Villa
2 Mrs Lee (under umbrella) at the races, 1920s
3 Mrs Lee wears her diamonds
4 Mrs Lee, dressed in her usual baju Shanghai, entertains friends
5 Kids on tricycles
6 Entertaining guests in the dining room, Mandalay Villa, 1930s
7 Bridal bed prepared for wedding of Lee Poh Neo and Lim Chong Pang
8 Casket of Lee Choon Guan in the main hall of Mandalay Villa, 1924
9 Wedding portrait of Lee Poh Neo and Lim Chong Pang, 1924

Beyond the increasingly suburban area of Katong and Siglap lay Chai Chee, Bedok and Changi. Here, the undulating terrain was put under cultivation by Chinese farmers (1). Such areas were largely developed by newer immigrants, many with families, who preferred to try small trades or farming, rather than subject their families to the crowded living conditions of Chinatown.

Living conditions in these rural areas were extremely primitive. There was no piped water or sewerage system, houses were basic wooden and *attap* structures and medical treatment could only be obtained by a trip to town.

The small villages in Chai Chee (2 and 8) and Bedok (6) were a place to meet, buy necessities and sell produce without venturing all the way downtown. Most farmers wore rough cotton trousers and tunics as did their wives, although the occasional white *tutup* was also seen.

Few main roads served the eastern portion of the island. Those that did, such as Changi (4) and Chai Chee (5) Roads, were still palm-embowered country lanes. The mouth of Bedok River (7) was a swamp punctuated by a few Chinese houses. All these photographs were taken by schoolteacher Lim Lam San (see pages 222–3) during the 1920s and 1930s. Each is captioned with the location.

1 Inscribed 'Vegetable Farm in Ulu Bedoh'
2 Chai Chee Village
3 Bedok swamp
4 Changi Road, 1920
5 Inscribed 'Road leading to Chye Chee'
6 Inscribed 'Kampong at Bedoh corner'
7 Inscribed 'Mouth of the Bedoh River'
8 Chai Chee Village

6

7

8

There were many ways an enterprising individual could make a living on the island. Artisans and craftsmen produced many of the basic necessities before the age of machinery. It was a tough life, however, requiring an entrepreneurial spirit, frugality, self-reliance and lots of hard work.

Bricks (3 and 4), baskets (5) and ceramic pots (2) were all made by hand in small workshops. Skills were either brought by immigrants from mainly agrarian home-lands, or learned from a *shifu*, or master, although the goal was usually to work for one's self. Most of the businesses were family-based, with work and living space fused into one. Hawking cooked food (10) required few overheads but offered the prospect of a good livelihood. Selling vegetables in the street (11) was a job often carried out by women.

Ships and *tongkang* were made in the village of Tanjong Rhu (7), while young *samsui* women (9) became a common sight on construction sites in the 1930s. The women, from the Sam Sui district in Guangdong Province, wore costumes of black trousers, blue tops and a red cloth wrapped to form a distinctive and protective headgear.

1 Inscribed '*Spreading out the* ikan bilis *to Dry*'
2 *Making Indian pots*
3–4 *Making cement bricks by hand*
5 Inscribed '*The Hen Coup Weaver*'
6 Inscribed '*Nipah leaves for making* daun rokok'
7 *Shipbuilder's yard, Tanjong Rhu*
8 *The blacksmith shop*
9 *A crew of* samsui *women*
10 Inscribed '*A vendor of eatables*'
11 Inscribed '*Buying goods off hawkers*'

1

2

3

4

5

6

7

8

9

10

11

1

2

3

4

Visitors to Singapore in the mid-1930s frequently recorded their amazement at the changes taking place around the island. One such account, by Robert Foran, reads, 'Beyond the heart of the city the former rubber estates are gradually but surely being absorbed in building developments. The erstwhile rubber-belt on the island is being thrust back relentlessly to make room for the urgent need for housing accommodation— and yet still more. Land in the heart of Singapore has soared in value until now it is worth more than a site in the vicinity of the Strand or Piccadilly. The plain truth of the matter is that building operations are unable to keep pace with the rapid growth of the population.'

One of the most significant projects was the Causeway which linked Singapore with Johor by road and rail in 1923 (5). Leonie Road, in the early 1930s, was a narrow road that ran through gently undulating landscape (2). Alkaff Gardens (3) was built by the wealthy Alkaff family, and thrown open to the public in 1929, offering boat rides and fishing on the lake. Further north, a tiger was shot in the jungle near Chua Chu Kang Road in 1928 (4), the slain predator with its hunters captured on film for posterity. Toa Payoh (6) was a farming community, while Seletar (8) was ideal for an adventurous outing. Pasir Panjang (1) was still a rustic kampong

By the 1930s, many Chinese were making the pilgrimage to Kusu Island (7), where the shrine to Tua Peh Kong, the Chinese God of Plenty, is housed. The pilgrimage, which still draws thousands, is made on the ninth day of the ninth month of the Chinese calendar for good health and prosperity.

1 Pasir Panjang Village, Wee Theam Seng, photographer, c. 1930
2 Leonie Road, late 1930s
3 Alkaff Gardens
4 Tiger hunting at Chua Chu Kang Village, 1928
5 The Causeway after completion in 1923
6 Kim Keat Road, Toa Payoh
7 Pilgrims at Kusu Island, 1930s
8 Inscribed 'Going up Seletar River'
9 Rubber works at Pasir Panjang, 1930s

The steep rise in land values bore heavily upon the Malays who wished to preserve a semi-rural way of life (1). When Mohammed Eunos bin Abdullah, a prominent figure in Malay social welfare organizations, became the first Malay Municipal Commissioner, he negotiated the formation of Kampong Melayu on a 240-hectare reserve beyond Geylang (see pages 220–1). He was also the first president of the Kesatuan Melayu Singapura, or Singapore Malay Union, whose leaders were mainly English-educated journalists, government officials and middle-class merchants.

While the members of the Persatuan Pensuda Bawuen Sungi Terta, or Boyanese Association, largely wore Western suits for a group photograph taken on 31 July 1940 (5), at wedding ceremonies (4) tradition prevailed. The bride wore *baju kerong*, the groom *baju seluar*. Women in the mid-1920s wore *kebaya panjang* which fell below the knee (3). The unusual photograph of a Bangawan opera scene (2) is from the 1930s. The modern costumes, including *sarong kebaya*, suggest that the show's themes were contemporary.

1

2

3

4

5

1

4

2

5

3

6

7

8

By 1931, there were 50,860 Indians in Singapore, constituting 9.2 per cent of the population. The rising tide of Indian nationalism was beginning to overcome differences of language and religion. Most communities were represented in meeting important visitors from India (4), including the famous poet Rabindranath Tagore (5) here photographed at the Siglap home of M. A. Namazie.

The 1930s also saw the formation of several associations, including the Indian Chamber of Commerce (8) in September 1935 and the Sindhi Merchants Association (2) whose members posed for a photograph taken in July 1941. Indian and Arab Muslims gathered for a photograph (6) at the home of the wealthy Alsagoff family. Tamil labourers, some of whom gathered for the visit of a religious leader (7), provided the labour for engineering projects, including the Causeway, Sembawang Dockyards and Kallang Airport, and were also involved in the building and servicing of the various military bases.

1

3

Special events and gatherings called for the services of a professional photographer. Members of the Chinese Chamber of Commerce, founded in 1906, posed for one such photograph in traditional garb when they gathered on 22 March 1922 at their Pavilion in the Malaya Borneo Exhibition to greet the Prince of Wales (4). Another group portrait (3), taken in the Chamber's headquarters in Hill Street (1), includes Lee Kong Chian (front row, second from left), one of the few dressed in a Western suit. Chamber members also posed outside the Great World Amusement Park at a Chinese trade fair in 1935 (6).

The prestigious Ee Ho Hean Club, or Singapore Chinese Weekly Entertainment Club (5), included Singapore's best known towkays among its members. A 1927 photograph (2) shows Mr Li Chen, Chinese Consul General in Singapore, posing with Lim Nee Soon (see pages 98–9), Wang Chung Wei, Tan Kah Kee, Khoo Kay Hian and Tay Sek Tin.

The expansion of Chinese education and increasing interest in the affairs of China boosted the sale of Chinese newspapers. By 1935, Aw Boon Haw's *Sin Chew Jit Poh* had a readership estimated at 30,000 in Malaya and Singapore, and Tan Kah Kee's *Nanyang Siang Pau* nearly 10,000. Among their readership were the growing number of educated middle-class Chinese, including clerks, merchants and their staffs, such as those posed in front of Lim Teck Lee High Class Shanghai Leather Trunk Merchant at Circular Road (7).

4

2

5

6

7

10

11

12

13

Fashions changed radically in the 1920s in response to a host of influences. English education imparted Western ideas, while Hollywood introduced the flappers and movie vamps. Magazines, published in both Chinese (7) and English, helped disseminate the latest in fashion.

The style-conscious looked to Shanghai. There, the melting pot of East and West produced a new mode of dress, the *qipao*, or cheongsam. The earlier versions (4 and 6), were shorter, boxier and had the sleeves of a traditionally cut Chinese tunic. By the 1930s, a different version had emerged: body skimming, flattering but not fitting, made from new textiles, and with elegant short or capped sleeves, long slits and hems hovering at the ankles (3 and 8). Western wedding attire was also adopted (12) but with variations, including an East–West fusion (11). High heels and cigarette cases became the epitome of sophistication, but perhaps the ultimate in liberation was the embracing of the swimming costume (1).

Among men, traditional modes of dress, including the white *tutup* (2), gradually disappeared, replaced by well-cut suits, both single- and double-breasted, in dark colours or tropical whites (9 and 10).

239

1

2

3

Prominent among the Straits Chinese community leaders was Song Ong Siang (1), a Queen's Scholar who graduated in law at Cambridge University, and the first Chinese to be admitted to the Singapore bar. He is also remembered for his book, *One Hundred Years' History of the Chinese in Singapore* (see page 172).

Of the Peranakan rites of passage, none was as lavish as the wedding (2–5). The couple were introduced by a matchmaker, and the traditions surrounding the 12-day ritual were so complex that special wedding personnel had to be engaged.

The remaining photographs are from the family albums of Chia Chin Siang, and they record the lifestyle of an affluent Straits Chinese family during the 1920s and 1930s. A young Master Chia posed for his father, Chia Keng Tye, with a new outboard motor (6). The Chia family lived in Rosedale (7) in Devonshire Road, and kept a seaside bungalow in Pasir Panjang (8). Chia Keng Tye was a man of many hobbies. He maintained several cars (11) and a fleet of fishing boats, and was the first Chinese to build a private tennis court at home. He was also an amateur musician, who founded a small orchestra, and an avid photographer.

4

5

6

7

9

8

10

11

12

13

14

15

1

2

The booming economy,
the development of a
more complex administration
and the opening of military
bases brought in greater
numbers of Europeans, many
of whom enjoyed the gay
social life (5, 7 and 9). Most
school-aged children were
shipped home to school,
although enough remained to
throw fancy dress parties (3).
Sir Cecil Clementi (1) served
as Governor of the Straits
Settlements in 1930–34.
He was succeeded by Sir
Shenton Thomas (2).

The Eurasian community
traced their ancestry to
diverse antecendents, but
had strong Singaporean
roots. By 1931, there were
almost 7,000 Eurasians,
three-quarters of whom were
born in Singapore. They were
well represented in the
middle ranks of the civil
service, where their English
education gave them an
advantage. Other prosperous
minorities included the
Armenians (6) and Jews (8).

3

4

5

7

8

9

10

6

243

1

2

3

4

5

6

9

7

8

10

11

12

13

No two family albums are identical, yet somehow they are all alike. The invention of affordable and easy-to-use cameras stimulated people to take pictures without any formal training, many of them in the course of an ordinary day. Free from the encumbrances and limitations of the professional, and without any preconceived notions about photography, the amateur was free to choose his or her viewpoint, angle and subject matter.

Familiar surroundings and company were far more conducive to relaxed poses and natural expressions. What is so appealing about these early snapshots of babies, outings with friends, leisure activities and loved ones is their relaxed, informal atmosphere and the sheer ordinariness of the scene: a mother crossing the road with her infant (1), music at home (2 and 8), outings at the beach (9) or in the park (5 and 11) and children fooling around for the benefit of the camera (10).

CHAPTER 4

TOWARDS NATIONHOOD
1941–1965

The atmosphere was apprehensive and the air was filled with the stench of death on Chinese New Year, 15 February 1942. The unthinkable had happened. Singapore, Britain's 'impregnable fortress', the bastion of her Eastern Empire, had fallen into the hands of the Japanese. With water supplies running dangerously low, the British had capitulated and signed the surrender document late that afternoon, in the makeshift Japanese headquarters set up in the Ford Factory on Bukit Timah Road. The following morning, Japanese soldiers marched victoriously into the city. Singapore was renamed Syonan, or 'light of the south', and clocks were set to Tokyo time.

The Japanese Occupation started brutally, and is remembered as a time of hardship and deprivation. British military and civilians were rounded up and marched off to POW camps. All Chinese were subjected to the mass screening exercise known as Sook Ching. The lucky ones were issued with identification passes, while countless others were imprisoned, tortured or executed. Private homes and cars were seized by the Japanese for their own use. Basic foodstuffs, including rice, became scarce. Rationing was a fact of life. Prices skyrocketed due to the scarcity of goods, leading to a flourishing black market. Although the Japanese wooed the Indians and favoured the Malays, anyone could be tortured on the mere suspicion of disrespect to Japanese authority. The brutality of the Kempeitai, the Japanese Military Police, kept people in a perpetual state of tension and fear.

As the war turned against them in early 1945, the Japanese prepared to defend Singapore to the bitter end. The possibility of a bloody battle, however, evaporated when the Americans dropped a pair of deadly atomic bombs on Hiroshima and Nagasaki on 6 and 9 August 1945, respectively. On 15 August, the Japanese formally surrendered. Three weeks later, British warships and Commonwealth troops steamed into Keppel Harbour to a tumultuous welcome. For the next six months, Singapore was placed under the British military administration. The war was over, but the problems it engendered—poverty, hunger, unemployment and an acute housing shortage—would take many years to solve.

The fall of Singapore was the first in a series of dramatic events which marked the road to independence in 1965. Until the Japanese Occupation, British rule went unquestioned. Colonial policies on education, language and citizenship had stifled the emergence of any sense of a shared destiny and identity. The major events in Asia during the first four decades of the 20th century—the humiliating decay of the Chinese Empire at the hands of European imperialists, the Chinese Revolution of 1911, the struggles between the Chinese Communist Party (CCP) and the Kuomintang, the Indian independence movement and, finally, the Japanese invasion of Manchuria in 1931—had stirred up strong feelings of Chinese and Indian nationalism as people continued to identify with their countries of origin.

After the war, the British were no longer regarded as invincible. Colonialism was crumbling in the face of rising nationalistic feelings in Asia and Africa. Newly independent countries in Asia were acquiring a voice of their own in world affairs under charismatic leaders such as Pandit Nehru and President Sukarno, and through forums like the first Afro–Asia Conference, which was held in

ABOVE *Balestier Primary School, 1958. With one of the highest birth rates in the world, Singapore's population swelled in the 1950s. The weight of the numbers was deeply felt.*
FACING PAGE *In a scene often repeated during the 1960s, Lee Kuan Yew visits constituents, here on the Southern Islands in 1966.*

balanced, with a larger proportion of women, children and old people. Male adults made up half the population in 1931, but only one-third in 1947. The revelation of an unexpectedly high proportion of locally born Singaporeans strengthened the argument for self-government.

The British intended to introduce self-rule to Singapore gradually. The first ever election was held in 1948 to fill six seats in the Legislative Assembly. The pace of change accelerated with the acceptance of the Rendel Constitution, which paved the way for a popular election on 2 April 1955 for a majority of representatives to the Legislative Assembly. The Labour Front captured 10 seats, and formed the first elected government of Singapore with prominent lawyer David Marshall as the first Chief Minister. Marshall was frustrated by his status as a figurehead while real power remained in the hands of the colonial government. Then, having pledged that he would not stay in office if he failed in his bid for self-government, he was forced to resign. His successor was Lim Yew Hock, who led the third all-party mission to London in 1958, where a constitutional agreement was reached for a State of Singapore with full powers of self-government.

Among the new political parties contesting the 1955 elections was the People's Action Party (PAP). It was formed in 1954 by a group of young men who had returned to Singapore in the early 1950s after studying in British universities. They were committed to the eradication of British colonialism and immediate independence for Singapore through union with Malaya. The group included the brilliant Cambridge-educated Lee Kuan Yew, economist and former civil servant Dr Goh Keng Swee, university lecturer Dr Toh Chin Chye and journalist S. Rajaratnam. English-educated,

Outdoor live Chinese broadcast of a football match at the Jalan Besar Football Ground, early 1950s. The first broadcast of the British Malayan Broadcasting Corporation took place in 1937. Postwar, Radio Malaya broadcast in four languages: English, Malay, Tamil and Chinese.

Bandung, Indonesia, in 1955. In 1949, Mao Ze Dong defeated the Kuomintang and unified China under communist rule. This, coupled with the ability of the Chinese army to fight the Americans to a stalemate in Korea, enormously enhanced the prestige of China among the Chinese everywhere.

With the end of the British military administration on 31 March 1946, Singapore reverted to being a Crown Colony. Malacca and Penang, which together with Singapore had formed the Straits Settlements, were absorbed into the Malayan Union. Singapore's exclusion was largely due to the fact that its huge Chinese majority would tip the racial balance against the Malays. The exclusion remained when, in 1948, the Federation of Malaya Agreement was adopted. This safeguarded the position of the Malays through preferential treatment and special rights, and limited the number of non-Malays to whom citizenship was granted. To many in Singapore, however, independence and merger with Malaysia were inseparable.

Singapore's population was now nearing the 1 million mark. The 1947 census counted 938,144 inhabitants, comprising a cosmopolitan mix of about 78 per cent Chinese, 12 per cent Malays and Indonesians, 7 per cent Indians and 3 per cent Eurasians and other small minorities. The population was less transitory and more

By the time Singapore's second civil airport opened at Paya Lebar in 1955, much of the excitement of aviation's pioneering days had dissipated. Work on a jet apron and the new passenger terminal had begun in 1961. The latter officially opened on 2 May 1964.

Chia Chin Siang photographed his wife and children in front of the Kranji War Memorial. Chia married in 1941 and survived the war, but his brother-in-law, Tan Jin Hoe, disappeared at a Sook Ching centre. Tan's name was engraved on the memorial.

of middle-class origins and with scant political experience, they faced the challenge of drumming up support from the masses, who were mostly uneducated and non-English speaking. Moreover, the Malayan Communist Party, with its efficient organizational and propaganda skills, was increasingly active and popular. The PAP declared itself non-communist—neither for nor against communism. When full elections came in 1959, the PAP scored a stunning victory, winning 43 out of 51 seats for Singapore's first self-governing Legislative Assembly, and Lee Kuan Yew became Prime Minister.

The communists, led by Lim Chin Siong and Fong Swee Suan, were also active after 1954. Using legally established non-communist organizations as fronts to further their cause, they infiltrated trade unions, Chinese middle schools, social organizations and political parties. They exploited issues to serve their own ends. By the time the communist leaders were arrested in a crackdown in 1957, violent communist-organized strikes and demonstrations had become a common occurrence. After winning the 1959 elections, the PAP, fulfilling a campaign promise, sanctioned the release of communist leaders as a prerequisite to taking up office on 12 June 1959. The communists continued to stir up unrest, although a major blow was dealt in February 1963, when a security crackdown code named 'Operation Coldstore' resulted in the arrest of 113 prominent pro-communist politicians and trade unionists, including Lim and Fong. Communist agitation in the form of industrial strikes and school boycotts, however, continued into 1967.

The newly elected government faced many urgent problems, especially in regard to the provision of jobs, education and housing for a swelling population. Singapore's population was growing rapidly due to a sharp decline in mortality, an increasing birth rate and the migration of people from Malaya. At the time of the 1957 census, the island was divided into the city and the rural area encompassing Katong, Serangoon, Bukit Panjang, Jurong and the Southern Islands. A steady flow of residents from the overcrowded city into the outlying districts had created fairly sizable suburbs. Still, 63 per cent of the population still resided in the city, where alarming densities of up to 142,176 persons per square kilometre were recorded.

Even as the government negotiated merger with and separation from Malaysia (see pages 320–1), it began the formidable task of developing a sense of belonging amongst Singaporeans, irrespective of ethnic origins. Singapore's own national flag, anthem and crest were introduced soon after the installation of Yusof bin Ishak as Singapore's first local Head of State. Malay, Chinese, Tamil and English were all made official languages. Changes in the education system were implemented to promote amongst students a sense of being Singaporean regardless of their language stream. A Ministry of Culture was set up to create new opportunities for the three main ethnic groups to develop an appreciation for one another's cultures. The Ministry was also charged with photographing events, ranging from open air multicultural concerts to the visits of the Prime Minister to his constituents. These photographs together with scenes of the city, the island and portraits of people, capture as vividly as words a fascinating era in Singapore's history.

New goals and pursuits. Women, such as this Malayan Airways stewardess (left), formed an increasingly important part of Singapore's workforce. In sports, the Malayan team, which included Wong Peng Soon (right), scored a stunning victory when they won the 1949 Thomas Cup.

1

Although China and Japan had been at war since July 1937, and Europe since September 1939, the threat of war in Southeast Asia seemed remote to most people in early 1941. In any case, Singapore was popularly regarded as an 'impregnable fortress', protected to the north by the thick jungles of the Malay Peninsula and to the south by massive gun installations hugging the coast. Confidence in the ability of the British to defend the island was high. The arrival of additional Indian, British (3) and Australian troops in early 1941 reinforced a false sense of security. The only local military units were four battalions of the Straits Settlements Volunteer Corps led by British officers, and a small civil defence force formed in 1939.

In October 1941, the war inched closer as the Japanese strengthened their position in southern Indochina—within striking distance of Singapore. On 1 December 1941, a state of emergency in Singapore was declared. Yet even at this late hour confidence ran high. The troop reinforcements, the authorities' pronouncements that all was well, and, finally, the arrival of the battleship HMS *Prince of Wales* (4) and the battle cruiser HMS *Repulse* on 2 December all continued to boost this confidence.

Singapore was caught off guard when the first Japanese air raid took place in the early hours of 8 December. The raid left 60 people dead and over 700 injured. The raid was part of a daring Japanese military offensive. At the same time, the Japanese had destroyed Pearl Harbour, invaded Hong Kong and the Philippines and landed forces in southern Thailand as well as in Kota Bharu. By the evening of 8 December, the Kota Bharu airfield was in Japanese hands. Two days later, on 10 December, Japanese torpedo bombers sank HMS *Prince of Wales* and HMS *Repulse* off the east coast of Malaya. The ships had left Singapore in the hope of intercepting the invading Japanese forces, but without air cover they proved easy targets for Japanese bombers.

Despite the official opposition to evacuation, Europeans and wealthy Asians began removing their families in the final days (6). But for many it was too late; Japanese planes controlled the skies—evacuation boats were easy to spot from the air.

---

1 Barbed wire placed around the north coast of Singapore
2 Local recruits are enlisted for defence
3 British troops landing, c. 1941–2
4 Arrival of HMS **Prince of Wales** *at Singapore Harbour,*
  2 December 1941
5 Tamil labourers survey damage to a building after the first Japanese
  bombing raid, 8 December 1941
6 Quayside scene as women and children evacuate, 8–13 February 1942
7 Mourning the death of a child killed in the first Japanese air raid,
  8 December 1941

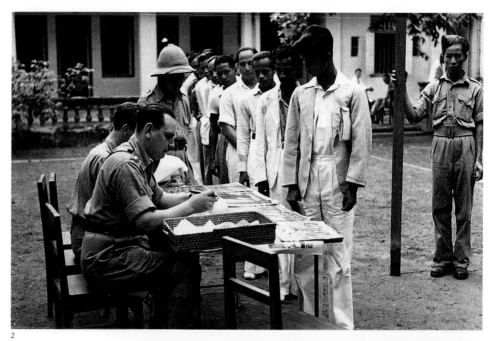

2

3

4

5

6

7

By late January 1942, Singapore was under intense air attack. The streets swelled with refugees. An estimated 150–200 people died each day, with entire families wiped out. Many buildings were destroyed.

On Sunday, 1 February, the Japanese began shelling Singapore. Unlike bombings, these attacks could not be signalled by sirens. Low flying Japanese airplanes targeted oil tanks, water reserves, airfields and the docks. With the Japanese just across the Causeway, the British military command ordered the destruction of installations and property that might help the Japanese war effort. The naval base was partially destroyed (3) and abandoned. By the time the Japanese crossed the Causeway, large areas of the city had been reduced to rubble, the streets were marked by gaping holes, the docks were in ruins and the city littered with burnt and abandoned vehicles. Churches, halls and hotels were turned into hospitals.

ABOVE *A city under siege. View from Cathay Building, 3 February 1942*
1 *Firefighters and a debris-filled street after an air attack,*
   3 February 1942
2 *Smoke arises from a demolished building at Rochor Canal Road,*
   3 February 1942
3 *Destruction of naval yards, February 1942*

1

2

3

4

5

The British boasted more troops, but the Japanese were far better equipped with tanks and aircraft. Lieutenant General Percival, the General Officer Commanding Malaya, had over 80,000 troops, but no tanks. At the start of the war, he had over 150 aircraft, but these were inferior and were grounded in the Japanese attacks on the airfields. Total Japanese combat strength was 67,000 soldiers supported by 150 tanks and 560 aircraft.

On 10 December 1941, the British began their retreat down the Malay Peninsula. On the morning of 31 January 1942, they blew up the Causeway, and withdrew to Singapore for the final showdown. Just hours later, Japanese troops had moved into Johor Bahru. On the night of 8 February, the first Japanese troops landed on the northwest coast of Singapore. After repairing the Causeway, they marched into Singapore, and, by 16 February, were all over the city.

1 *Japanese forces entering Singapore, 9–14 February 1942*
2 *A Japanese tank on Orchard Road*
3 *The Japanese march into Raffles Place after the British surrender, 14–15 February 1942*
4 *British soldiers are marched to Changi*
5 *A British soldier on a motorbike is questioned by a Japanese soldier the day following the surrender, 16 February 1942*

1

2

3

On 15 February 1942, Lieutenant General Percival reluctantly decided to surrender. Flying the white flag, he led the small British contingent (1) to the Ford Factory on Bukit Timah where the Japanese had already set up headquarters. The meeting with Lieutenant General Yamashita was tense (2 and 3). The Japanese insisted on immediate and unconditional surrender. Their only concession was to agree not to enter the city until the following morning. At 7.50 p.m., the surrender was concluded. It was the first day of the Lunar New Year, 15 February 1942. Winston Churchill labelled the fall of Singapore 'the worst disaster and largest capitulation in British history'.

Three days after the surrender, on 18 February, the Japanese launched Sook Ching, a bloody purge of Chinese who had supported the war effort in China and participated in anti-Japanese activities. Chinese men between the ages of 18 and 50 were required to report to screening centres (4), and interrogated. The screening was arbitrary, and unlucky ones were taken away in lorry loads to Changi, Punggol and Pulau Blakang Mati (Sentosa) where they were shot. It is estimated that as many as 50,000 were killed in this exercise. Other races were not spared. Sikh soldiers who had cooperated with the British were also executed (5 and 6).

1 *British surrender deputation, led by Lt Gen Percival, Brig. Torrance, Brig. T. K. Newbigging, Maj. Cyril Wild, and Col. Sugita walk to the Ford Factory. One brigadier carries the Union Jack and the other the white flag, 15 February 1942*
2 *Signing of the surrender document*
3 *Tense negotiations at the Ford Factory between Lt Gen A. E. Percival, Commander of the British Forces in Singapore, and Lt Gen Tomoyuki Yamashita, 15 February 1942*
4 *Stolen snapshot. A secretly taken photograph of the mass screening exercise known as Sook Ching*
5 *Sikh soldiers of the British defence forces executed by Japanese soldiers, 1942*
6 *The final act: a Japanese soldier bayonets one of his victims*
7 *British troops surrendering*

1943年

ラッフルス博物館図書館

博物館に今では
スタンフォード・ラッフルスの
銅像

2

3

4

5

6

7

8

The Japanese renamed Singapore Syonan or 'light of the south'. A Speak Japanese Campaign was initiated. Lessons in 'Nippon-Go' were offered at the numerous Japanese language schools, called Gakko (5), which were established. Japanese was also taught in all primary schools; secondary education ground to a halt. The statue of Sir Stamford Raffles (6) was removed to the Shonan Museum (1), while a Shinto shrine was built by POWs at MacRitchie Reservoir (7).

The Japanese encouraged the Indian nationalist movement, and supported the formation of the Indian Independence League and the Indian National Army (INA) with Captain Mohan Singh as its General. INA enrolment rose sharply after the arrival of Subhas Chandra Bose, who whipped up the crowds' fervour at a rally on the Padang in July 1943 (8).

The standard of living deteriorated rapidly. As an occupied port, Singapore lost her free port and trade status. Food became scarce, and most people lived hand-to-mouth.

1 A page from the past documents the Raffles Museum and Library when it was renamed the Shonan Museum. The main photograph shows Dr Haneda, Marquis Tokugawa and Secretaries Sugawata, Tachida, Onori, Yoshu and Ishii posing outside the Museum, July 1943
2 Japanese soldiers and members of the Chew family at Rosedale, Killiney Road
3 Japanese soldiers pose at Kallang Airport, March 1942
4 Japanese soldiers on the steps of the Municipal Building
5 Students of a Gakko School, 1942
6 Removal of the Raffles Statue from Victoria Place to the Shonan Museum, 13 September 1942
7 Japanese Shinto shrine, the Syonan Jinja, a POW project at MacRitchie Reservoir, 1942
8 Subhas Chandra Bose and Japanese Premier Tojo salute at an Indian National Army parade on the steps of the Municipal Building, 5 July 1943

1

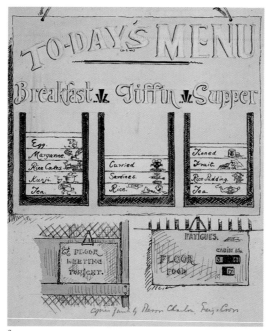

2

3

4

5

6

7

8

9

10

11

12

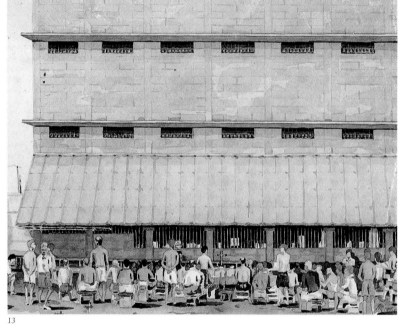

13

14

W. R. Haxworth was Superintendent of Traffic Police from 1929 to 1954. He not only survived incarceration during the Japanese Occupation, but chronicled life as a POW with a remarkable sense of humour. Haxworth's 400 watercolours and drawings are a remarkable collection given the severe lack of paper and other supplies in prison.

1 Changi Prison, 24 November 1942
2 Today's menu, 4 February 1942
3 View of Cell 17, Changi Prison, 21 March 1943
4 Inscribed 'Home—My Corner', Changi Prison, 1 January 1942
5 Inscribed 'Wall Cupboard', Changi Prison, 6 June 1942
6 Inscribed 'On Sunday 5th July 1942 a father celebrated his son Christopher's first birthday'
7 Inscribed 'Hospital Hill, Sime Road Camp', 19 June 1945
8 Inscribed 'Rain!', Changi Prison, 1 January 1945
9 Japanese guards, 23 April 1945
10 Rough sketches, 23 April 1945
11 Inscribed 'John—promoted to road sweeper as from 1.1.45'
12 Inscribed 'Hut 101, Sime Road Camp', 28 January 1945
13 Changi Prison, 15 November 1942
14 Night scene, 25 December 1942

1

2

3

4

5

6

7

8

By the end of 1944, the tide of war had begun to turn against the Japanese. The Allied Forces' bombing of Japan culminated in the dropping of the first ever atomic bombs over Hiroshima and Nagasaki. Within days, on 15 August 1945, Emperor Hirohita surrendered unconditionally.

In Singapore, British warships arrived on 5 September to a tumultuous carnival-like welcome. Four days later, on 12 September, General Seishiro Itagaki surrendered to Admiral Lord Louis Mountbatten, Supreme Allied Commander in Southeast Asia, in the Council Chamber of the Municipal Building (1).

Japanese soldiers were marched to prison camps and dispatched as working parties. A War Crimes Commission was formed to investigate the atrocities committed by the Japanese. Altogether, 135 were tried and convicted.

People both living and dead were acknowledged for their contributions to the defence of Singapore and the anti-Japanese resistance. Lim Bo Seng, one of the leaders of Force 136, was given a posthumous memorial service on 13 January 1946 (5). Chin Peng, the guerrilla commander of the Malayan People's Anti-Japanese Army (MPAJA), was awarded the Burma Star (8) on 6 January 1946.

Contrary to expectations, the return of the British did not result in a quick improvement in living conditions. There was widespread hunger and malnutrition. The colonial authorities established 'People's Restaurants' in 1946 (6 and 7) to provide subsidized meals.

1 *Signing of the Japanese surrender document. Gen. Seishiro Itagaki and Adm. Lord Louis Mountbatten, Supreme Allied Commander in Southeast Asia, in the Council Chamber, Municipal Building, 12 September 1945*

2 *Japanese POWs clean up the Padang*

3 *Execution of Gen. Fukuei Shempei, Changi, April 1946*

4 *Cheering crowds of young Malayans welcome the British to Singapore, 5 September 1945*

5 *Mourners bow in silence at the funeral ceremony of war hero Col. Lim Bo Seng, Municipal Building, 13 January 1946*

6–7 *Food shortages, poverty and malnutrition were serious postwar problems. The first 'People's Restaurant' opened on 29 June 1946 and functioned until 1948, offering meals at subsidized rates.*

8 *Adm. Lord Louis Mountbatten congratulates Malayan People's Anti-Japanese Army leader, Chin Peng, who was awarded both the Burma Star and the 1939–45 Star*

1

2

3

4

At the war's end, the town was dirty, shabby and neglected. The roads were full of potholes; buildings were run down. Water, electricity, gas and telephone services had all deteriorated. Gradually, however, the main business areas were spruced up, although the buildings along Raffles Quay (2) still appeared much as they had at the turn of the century. Cecil Street and Robinson Road (9) consisted of three- and four-storey shophouses. The first skyscrapers, the Bank of China (1) and the Asia Insurance Building, stood in stark contrast to their predominantly Victorian neighbours. The Bank of China was designed by Palmer and Turner, was constructed in 1954–5, and was the first building to be centrally air-conditioned. The Asia Insurance Building, visible in the background of the view of Raffles Place (8), was designed by British-trained architect Ng Keng Siang in 1948, but was completed only in 1955. At 18 storeys, it was for many years Singapore's tallest building.

Singapore was proclaimed a city by a Royal Charter on 22 September 1951. The Municipal Council was henceforth known as the City Council, and the Municipal Building as City Hall.

1 *Battery Road with the Bank of China under construction, c. 1954*
2 *Raffles Quay*
3 *Empress Place*
4 *Collyer Quay from the sea*
5 *Floods in Cecil Street, 1948*
6 *Flooding at Circular Road*
7 *Stamford Road and Hill Street with Eu Court in the background*
8 *Raffles Place*
9 *Robinson Road*
10 *Mid-19th century buildings, Raffles Place*

5

7

8

9

6

10

265

1

In the 1930s, a major land reclamation was carried out in anticipation of the expansion of downtown. This substantial parcel of land (3), with Shenton Way as its main trunk road, then stood empty for nearly 30 years. The first structure built on it was the Singapore Polytechnic campus, which was completed in 1958 and used by the school until 1979. Next to be erected was the building that housed the National Trade Union Congress and the Singapore Conference Hall, both completed in 1965. (In 1971 the Conference Hall played host to the first British Commonwealth Heads of State Conference to be held outside London.) Otherwise the land was used as a car park by day, becoming a popular gathering area for hawkers by night.

The combination of car park and hawker stalls was also a characteristic of New Bridge Road (1) with its profusion of hoardings and petrol pumps. Rochor Canal (2) flowed through the grassy banks at the junction of Selegie and Serangoon Roads. From the quiet grounds of the Chinese Chamber of Commerce (4), the steeple of the Armenian Church could be seen.

1 New Bridge Road, c. 1960
2 Rochor Canal at junction of Selegie and Serangoon Roads, late 1950s
3 Shenton Way and Robinson Road, c. 1957
4 An urban landmark. Steeple of the Armenian Church as seen from the
  front garden of the Chinese Chamber of Commerce.
5 Colombo Court, behind Supreme Court, 1957

2

3

4

COLOMBO COURT

5

1

2

3

4

5

Orchard Road (6) was no longer a country lane, but its mostly two-storey shophouses were still shaded by large trees. This view looks south from the junction of Cairnhill Road towards the entrance to Emerald Hill Road. Among the postwar additions to the line of fashionable shops and restaurants was Prince's Building (10), which housed Prince's, a restaurant described in an early 1950s guidebook as 'amongst the more exclusive' of Singapore's nightspots. The Rediffusion Building on Clemenceau Avenue (8) was built by Palmer and Turner in 1948–9. Stamford Road landmarks included Malayan Publishing House (MPH) (4) and the newly completed National Library (7).

The idea for a free public library was enthusiastically discussed in the early 1950s, but the foundation stone was only laid in 1957 by rubber magnate and philanthropist Lee Kong Chian. Mr Lee had pledged a generous donation of $375,000 towards its foundation, on the condition that it carry books in the Asian languages and which are representative of the cultures of Singapore. Upon completion in July 1960, the building was described as 'out of character', 'intimidating', 'forbidding' and 'a jumble of architectural sections lumped together to form a haphazard whole'. More importantly, perhaps, the interior functioned well and the library was an immediate success.

1 *Stamford Road, early 1950s*
2 *Telephone pole and cables, 1954*
3 *Coleman Street*
4 *Stamford Road and MPH Building, mid-1950s*
5 *City traffic, South Bridge Road, 1962*
6 *Orchard Road, early 1950s*
7 *National Library, 1962*
8 *Rediffusion Building, Clemenceau Avenue, 1962*
9 *Radio Singapore Building, Caldecott Hill, 1962*
10 *Prince's Building, Orchard Road, early 1950s*

6

7

8

9

10

1

2

3

4

5

6

7

8

9

10

11

Almost anything was for sale in the 'Emporium of the East'. The tiny one-room shops of Change Alley (9) had an atmosphere all their own and were famous for their profusion of goods—and services. Here, touts changed money, tour guides offered to take visitors to places not mentioned in guidebooks, and tailors promised a stylish sharkskin suit in an afternoon.

The more upmarket Arcade (8) extended from Collyer Quay to Raffles Place and was, essentially, the city's first indoor shopping centre. Its small boutiques catered mainly to office workers, selling a great variety of imported goods, from toiletries to sports equipment. Shoppers and workers could refresh themselves with pastries and cool drinks in the popular air-conditioned Cold Storage Milk Bar.

C. K. Tang moved to Orchard Road (7). However, most Singaporeans did their shopping—whether for textiles, new clothes, books, sundries or household items—outdoors at street stalls, along five-foot ways and in markets.

1 *Clothing stalls at Happy World*
2 *Indian roadside stall*
3 *Textile stall, South Bridge Road*
4 *Joo Chiat Market*
5 *British servicemen shopping near their base, early 1950s*
6 *Pavement library at Queen Street*
7 *C. K. Tang, Orchard Road, early 1960s*
8 *The Arcade, Singapore's first indoor shopping mall*
9 *Change Alley where' everything from hatpins to electronic toys are on sale'*
10 *Girls selected as Constitutional Exposition Receptionists, 1959*
11 *Samsui woman admiring the unobtainable*

1

2

3

4

5

6

7

8

9

10

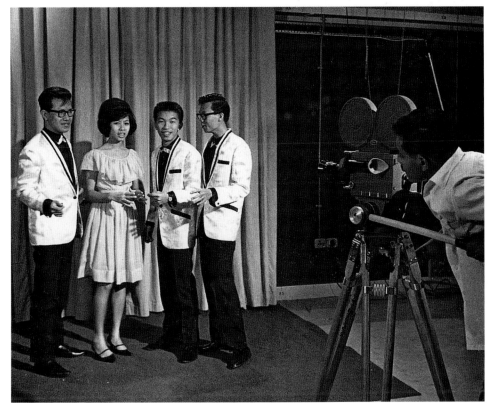

11

A small but active circle of artists in the 1950s were searching for a Singaporean aesthetic. A 1952 field trip to Bali (2) turned out to be the inspiration which enabled them to crystalize that endeavour. The Society of Chinese Artists (1) was founded in 1935. Movies were a main form of entertainment, with large cinema halls such as Lido (10) catering to the crowds. After 1963 though, competition came from television (11).

1 *Executive Committee of the Society of Chinese Artists, 1954*
2 *Pioneer artists. During the Bali field trip in 1952, Liu Kang, Chen Chong Swee, Chen Wen Hsi and Cheong Soo Pieng posed with artist Le Mayeur and his Balinese wife.*
3 *Violinist Goh Soon Tjoe with family, mid-1950s*
4 *Lee Kong Chian visits the Society of Chinese Artists' annual exhibition, mid-1950s*
5 *Malcolm McDonald, High Commissioner for Southeast Asia, at the Society of Chinese Artists' annual exhibition at the old Chinese Chamber of Commerce, mid-1950s*
6 *Writer Han Su Yin, lawyer David Marshall and Cathay Cinema's Dato Loke Wan Tho at a function, mid-1950s.*
7 *Chen Chong Swee's* Stone and Bamboo
8 *Georgette Chen's* Festival Table
9 *Cheong Soo Pieng at work in Flat 72, Cathay Building*
10 *Lido Cinema, 1960*
11 *TV Singapura. When the first broadcast took place on 15 February 1963, thousands of spectators crowded in front of Victoria Memorial Hall to catch a glimpse of the television sets lined up on wooden planks.*

1

The river remained as essential to trade after the war as it was before. Crowded with *tongkang* ferrying goods to and from ships and godowns, lined with dilapidated buildings, its quays served as living room and community centre for ageing and illiterate coolies who depended on storytellers for amusement (5). In *See Singapore*, one of the earlist illustrated books on Singapore, Han Su Yin vividly described the Singapore River as 'a broad, slimy, refuse-laden waterway, smelling of commerce, Asia and the two jungles (the vegetable and the human). But it is enormously alive, vibrant and forceful, unforgettable with life … The godowns of the trading companies abut on to the river. Out of them come the crates and bales, baskets and boxes, to be laden on small craft which ply up and down.'

The river and its inhabitants were a popular subject for photographers in the 1950s. The old man of the River (1) is by Kathinka Fox who operated a studio selling albums of Singapore views. Coleman Bridge (3) and the upper reaches of the river (6 and 7) were photographed by Dr Carl Gibson-Hill who was then Director of the Raffles Museum and an avid photographer.

1 The old man of the River
2 South Boat Quay, 1952
3 Coleman Bridge and New Bridge Road
4 A timeless scene: unloading cargo along south Boat Quay
5 Storytelling along the river, 1960
6–7 Upriver views, early 1950s

3

2

4

5

6

7

It was from the sea that many new arrivals caught their first glimpse of Singapore. Vessels that did not dock at Keppel Harbour but remained at anchor offshore, in full view of the city, discharged their passengers into small boats for the run to Clifford Pier (1).

Until the war, port facilities had steadily improved. The Singapore Harbour Board, which was constituted in 1912, had immediately launched a building programme to upgrade port facilities. This included the construction of a detached mole to protect coastal vessels, the opening of the new King's Dock, land reclamation at Telok Ayer and the replacement of the wooden wharves with modern concrete structures. Modernization continued with improvements to lighthouses, signal stations and navigational aids. New equipment such as tugs, electric cranes and forklifts were also introduced over the years. Other significant developments were the birth of Pulau Bukom as an oil refinery and the setting up of shipyards at Sembawang.

These expansions were interrupted by World War II which destroyed 60 per cent of the warehouses and machinery. Sunken craft clogged the waters and businesses shut down. When trade resumed, it was proof of the port's resilience. Throughout the 1950s Singapore's main exports were rubber, tin and copra. Coconut oil, palm oil, tinned pineapple, sago flour, rattan and spices were also exported.

1 *Clifford Pier and Collyer Quay, 1962*
2 *Small sailing vessels, early 1950s*
3 *Loading of rubber at wharf, 1960*
4 *Cranes ease the work, Tanjong Pagar, 1962*
5 *Tanjong Rhu, early 1950s*
6 *Inscribed 'Kallang river ship repair', early 1950s*
7 *Passengers alighting from ship, 1957*
8 *Pilgrims returning from Mecca, 1949*

6

7

8

BENDEMEER VILLAGE
1957(?)

1

The housing shortage after the war reached critical proportions. No new housing had been erected during the Japanese Occupation. In 1947, the population approached the 1 million mark, more than double what it was 20 years before. Exorbitant sums were demanded for rent during the Occupation, forcing thousands to become squatters. Large numbers of primitive shacks were constructed around the edges of the town and beyond, such as in Bendemeer Village (1). Even as economic conditions returned to normal, many people continued to live in fire-prone wooden and zinc structures or in congested slums.

1 *Squatters' village in Bendemeer, c. 1957*
2 *Children bathing in a crèche, 1949*
3 *Studying at home, early 1950s*
4 *At the dinner table, 1956*
5–6 *Family portraits, 1952*
7 *A nonya in her kitchen, 1951*
8 *Prayers at the family altar, c. 1960*

2

3

4

5

6

7

8

1

2

3

In the first postwar report of the Singapore Improvement Trust, published in 1947, the chairman made a commitment 'to rehouse the people and to abolish the fearful slums of the town with their terrible overcrowding and their attendant evils of crime and disease'. As a first step, a committee was formed to inquire into housing problems and make recommendations. The population density of many parts of the city reached nearly 2,500 people to the hectare. This was due largely to landlords dividing and further subdividing rooms to squeeze in tenants. Generally, the worst overcrowding occurred in the most dilapidated buildings.

1 *Kampong Glam*
2 *Petain Road*
3 *Hari Raya shoppers at Arab Street, 1960*
4 *Sungei Road*
5 *Waterloo Street with steeple of Church of Our Lady of Lourdes in distance*
6 *Rochor Canal*
7–8 *Small traders at Thieves Market, Sungei Road, conducted a brisk
    business in second-hand goods.*

1

2

3

4

5

6

Some of the worst slums were in Chinatown where the tight grid of streets consisted almost entirely of two- and three-storey shophouses. These were originally intended to house only one or two families, but had been divided by partitions into a maze of cubicles, mostly without windows. Cubicles were roughly the size of two double beds. In a typical cubicle would live a family of seven or more. Many of the children slept on the floor, often under the bed. Possessions were kept in boxes that were placed on shelves. Food was kept in tiny cupboards hanging from the rafters. 'The turned up roofs, the squeezed tenement houses, the leprous walls of Chinatown; so much decrepitude condemned as unfit, yet which must go on lodging many thousands,' wrote Han Su Yin. 'Its walls sticky with the slime of years, its day-long banners of family washing thrusting out of every window, and its narrow, crumbling tenements which have a queer habit of falling down of their own accord, in a soft confusion of smothered dust and cries.'

Families confined to small cubicles used the five-foot way as a common area. Here children played, meals were eaten and friends met and chatted. An enormous variety of economic activities was also conducted on the five-foot way. With high unemployment and underemployment, there was a dependency on hawking and petty trading for a living.

1 North Boat Quay
2 Ang Siang Hill
3–4 In the heart of Chinatown: Temple Street and Trengganu Street
5 Hock Lam Street
6 Living room, dining room and playground. Lives were lived along the five-foot way

In its 32 years of existence, the Singapore Improvement Trust (SIT) constructed some 23,000 flats. There were, in addition, another 20,129 units of public housing managed by bodies such as the Public Works Department, the City Council and the Singapore Harbour Board. This fell far short of the housing needs of the population. The Housing Committee of 1947 had called for a Master Plan which would provide for satellite towns, industrial estates and land acquisition. However, no significant large scale building programme was initiated. Between 1947 and 1959, only one dwelling unit was built for every 16-person increase in the population.

FACING PAGE *Pagoda Street, mid-1950s*
1 *SIT flats, Upper Pickering Street*
2–4 *SIT flats in Tiong Bahru*

1

2

For many, it was not easy to make a living in the 1950s. Unemployment and underemployment were endemic. Some 20,000 job seekers were entering the labour market yearly. Trade, Singapore's main economic activity, could hardly absorb all the unemployed. Existing manufacturing industries were, on the whole, small establishments which employed only a small number of workers.

While most rubber (9) was exported, several firms manufactured rubber products such as shoes, bicycle tyres and tubes, hospital sheetings and implements for mining. Pineapple canning, prior to the Japanese Occupation, was the third largest industry after tin and rubber. After the war, it gradually picked up (3), and tinned pineapples were exported to Europe, Canada, New Zealand, India and the Middle East. There were numerous Chinese-owned sawmills (6) on the island, which catered partly to local consumption and partly to export. Timber came from the Malayan forests as well as Indonesia, Borneo and Thailand.

Other small scale enterprises produced basic necessities such as soap, biscuits, cooking oil, sauce, soft drinks, batteries (7) and shoes. Most of these manufacturers employed only a few workers. New industries included a net-making factory (10) that supplied the regional fishing industry.

1 Provision shop, 1954
2 Sundry shop, 1954
3 Inscribed 'Government canning officer Mr Cook discusses morning's fruit with factory manager', early 1950s
4 Co-op society, Kampong Melayu, 1958
5 Typesetting machines in The Straits Times Printing Works, early 1950s
6 Sawmill, 1955
7 Machine shop, 1956
8 Sewing piece goods
9 Rubber factory, early 1950s
10 Fishing net manufacturing, 1951

3

4

5

6

7

8

9

10

1

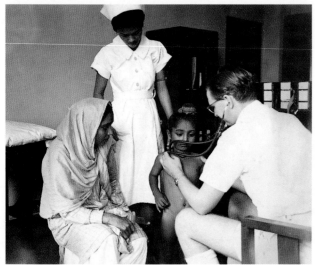

2

3

4

5

6

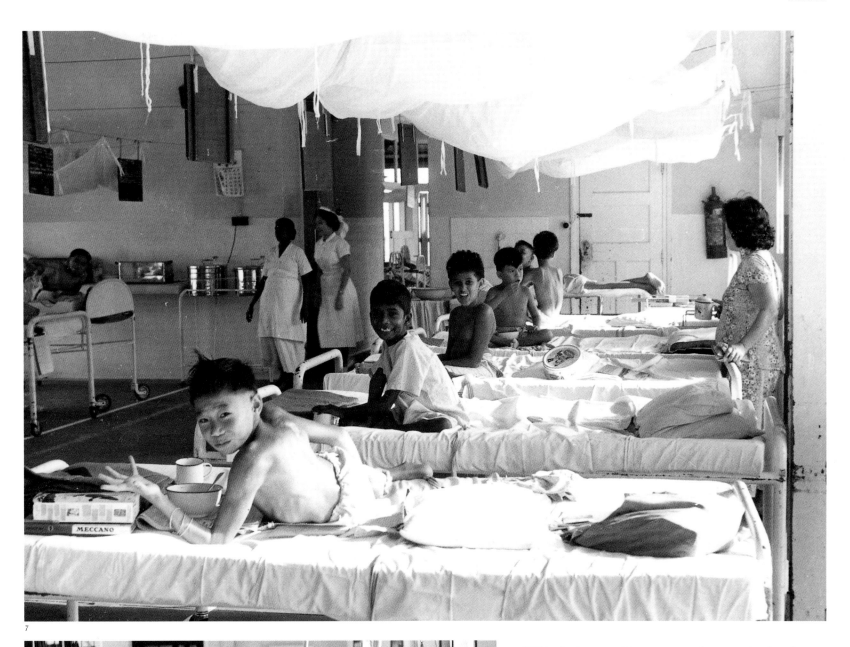

7

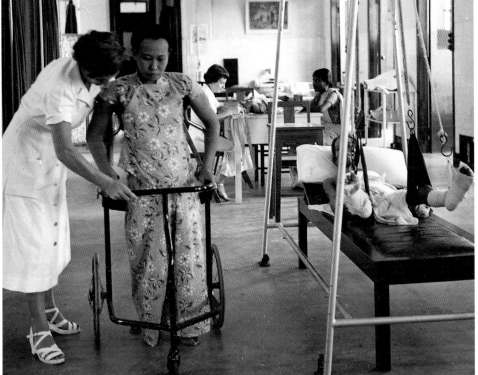

8

The death rate in 1945 was twice the prewar level, and hospitals were bare of equipment and medicines. Diseases caused by malnutrition and poverty were rampant. In June 1946, a Social Welfare Department was set up to deal with the postwar hardships, and, in 1951, a 10-year health plan was put into effect. This gave top priority to primary healthcare. New outpatient services were made available in rural districts, and a school of nursing opened at Singapore General Hospital (8).

St Andrew's Mission Hospital (7) moved into new premises in Tanjong Pagar in 1948, becoming a hospital for children. In May 1954, it opened a ward to treat children with tuberculosis of the bones and joints (7). Most of the patients were from the dank cubicles of nearby Chinatown. Parents were illiterate and superstitious of hospitals, and diseases often reached an advanced stage before the patients were admitted to hospital.

1 Children queue for milk, Radin Mas School, 1948
2 Child Welfare Clinic, 1950
3 Pulau Tekong Clinic, 1951
4 Fighting tuberculosis
5 Singapore General Hospital, early 1950s
6 Inoculation programme, 1957
7 St Andrew's Mission Hospital, 1950s
8 Singapore General Hospital, early 1950s

1

In 1945, the British reopened schools where, in addition to the normal intake, places were given to children who, because they had received no schooling during the Japanese Occupation, were overaged for their academic year.

English schools were of three distinct types: government, government-aided (run by religious organizations) and private, mainly vernacular, schools. The long-established schools continued to be the most prestigious, such as Raffles Institution (5) and Raffles Girls' School (6). To cope with the demand for education, more government schools were opened, mainly on the fringes of the Municipality and in the rural areas. But by 1959, the shortage of schools had become acute. There were places for only 85 per cent of children needing primary education and for only 23 per cent of those in need of secondary education.

Chinese education was also a major problem. English was the only official language, yet nearly half the school population was enrolled in Chinese-medium schools where the curriculum was primarily China-oriented, and, which, unlike English-medium schools, did not enjoy adequate support or full recognition. The teachers were poorly paid; Chinese school graduates could not secure jobs in the civil service nor gain entry into university.

In January 1953, Tan Lark Sye, a wealthy rubber merchant and industrialist, proposed the establishment of a Chinese University at a meeting of the Hokkien Huay Kuan. The proposal was met with suspicion by the colonial government, but they did not stop it. The Chinese community responded enthusiastically. The Hokkien Huay Kuan donated a large piece of land at Jurong and taxi drivers and trishaw riders even donated a day's earnings towards the University's building fund. Nanyang University (2) officially opened on 30 March 1958.

Raffles College became the University of Malaya (3), incorporating the old King Edward VII Medical School as the new Faculty of Medicine. Institutions founded at this time include Singapore Polytechnic, which started operating in 1957, and the Teachers' Training College, which opened in March 1950.

1 *Lee Kong Chian, philanthropist and patron of education*
2 *Entrance gate to Nanyang University, 1955*
3 *University of Malaya Convocation, 1951*
4 *Inside the classroom, 1950s*
5 *Raffles Institution, 1952*
6 *Raffles Girls' School*
7 *Convent girls*
8 *School boys*

2

3

4

5

6

7

8

1

These studies of everyday life are by the Sarawak-born, award-winning photographer K. F. Wong, one of several talented Southeast Asian photographers working in the 1950s.

In the 1930s, Wong studied art in Amoy where he was also a professional photographer's apprentice. When the war came to south China, he returned to Sarawak. With basic equipment and limited film, he began to shoot the peoples of the rivers and jungles, such as the Ibans and Dayaks. While best known for these portraits, he also visited Singapore over the years, camera in hand, and one of his temple scenes drew high praise at the Royal Photographic Society's 1950 exhibition in London.

Wong captured with great dignity the most ordinary of scenes—the trishaw rider reading his newspaper, men in a coffee shop, life along the five-foot ways. The old colonial city was then on the brink of enormous change, and Wong's photographs, 750 of which were acquired by the National Archives of Singapore in 1988, have become classics.

1 *Tai Tong Restaurant, 1963*
2 *Trishaw man, c. 1960*
3 *Market scene, early 1960s*
4 *Elgin Bridge, 1962*
5 *Pavement barber, 1963*
6 *Pavement hairdresser 1962*

2

3

4

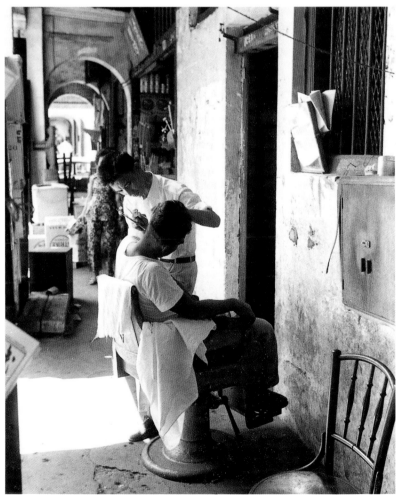

5

6

1

3

Outside the city limits much of the island was rural. From Jurong (6) to Changi, the landscape consisted of dairy (3) and vegetable (4) farms, Chinese squatter villages and Malay kampongs including Geylang Serai (7 and 9).

The warm waters around the island were fertile grounds for fishermen (8) who worked by night. Each night's catch was sold by auction early the next morning, with Chinese middlemen conducting the transactions. East Coast Road passed through Katong, with its sandy kampongs (2) and fashionable houses, and skirted the seafront (10) to Changi Point. On the way to Changi was Bedok, then, according to an early 1950s guide-book, 'another popular seaside resort to which Singaporeans flock on Sundays and on weekdays after nightfall'.

1 *Pasir Panjang Police Station, 1958*
2 *Hawker visits kampong, Katong, 1962*
3 *Dairy farm in Bukit Timah, 1962*
4 *Vegetable farm in Potong Pasir, 1962*
5 *Morning scene, Potong Pasir Village, 1959*
6 *Jurong farmer, 1954*
7 *Flood relief at Geylang Serai, 1954*
8 *A fisherman relaxes after a night of work, Katong beach, 1959*
9 *Geylang Serai, 1962*
10 *Katong beach, 1960*

4

2

5

6

7

8

9

10

1

Any ramble along the city's streets brought you face to face with the island's myriad hawkers. Many hawkers were regularly arrested and fined because they had no licences, which were limited in number. But with a living to be earned, these hawkers were soon on the road again. The unhygienic handling of food was, however, a constant health hazard.

The most famous night-time haunts for Chinese food were Bugis and Albert Streets. Bugis Street (1) was a favourite of sailors, transvestites and the patrons of cinemas and dance halls. Numerous stalls, crowded together in front of dilapidated shophouses and lit by kerosene lamps, offered a variety of succulent dishes. The most famous place for satay was the Satay Club (2), located off Beach Road. The freshest produce was on sale in Ellenborough Market (following pages) where hard earned money changed hands only after prolonged bargaining.

1 Bugis Street, 1962
2 Satay Club, Beach Road, 1962
3 Bugis Street hawker, 1962
4 Along the Singapore River, 1962
5 Joo Chiat Market, 1962
6 Coffee shop, 1962
7 Selegie Road stalls, 1963
8 Traditional cake and drinks stall, c. 1960

FOLLOWING PAGES
Ellenborough Market, 1950s

2

3

4

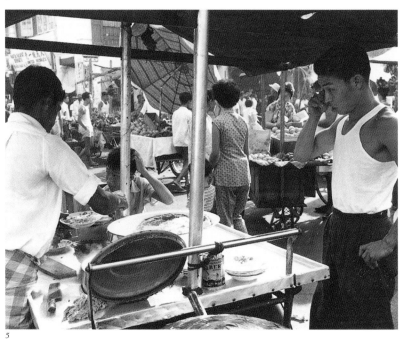

5

6

7

8

1

2

3

4

5

6

7

Postwar Singapopre's Malay population stood at 12 per cent of the island's 1.1 million people. Several of these photographs capture the bustle of Geylang and Eunos: a *songkok* stall at Geylang Market in 1963 (1); school girls in Joo Chiat Place, 1962 (6); and a kampong house in Jalan Eunos in 1949 (3). The other photographs reflect religious practices: pilgrims embarking on their voyage to Mecca, early 1950s (2); an elderly man coaching his grandson on the Koran in Katong, late 1950s (4); and women at a female circumcision ceremony, early 1950s (5).

Singapore's first Malayan-born Yang di-Pertuan Negara, Yusof bin Ishak (7), was installed on 3 December 1959. Born in Perak in 1910, he had been Editor-in-Chief and Managing Director of the *Utusan Melayu* newspaper for many years.

Between 1947 and 1957, the Indian population rapidly increased. Some two-thirds were migrants from the Federation of Malaya who were attracted to Singapore by the higher salaries and better opportunities. There was also an influx of northern Indians, particularly Sikhs and Sindhis, who emigrated in 1947–8 during the unrest which followed Indian independence and the partition of India and Pakistan. While most Indians, Pakistanis and Ceylonese (Sri Lankans) still looked with pride to their homelands, increasing numbers settled down in Singapore. It was still common practice for male Indian labourers to come on their own, and the proportion of women to men was smaller than in any of the other communities. The majority of Indians sent money to their families in India, travelling frequently between India and Singapore. The images here include Tamil coolies cleaning a boat (facing page); an Indian *dhoby* shop, early 1950s (1); musician Paul Abisheganaden (2); Thaipusam, 1948 (3); a barber in Geylang, 1963 (4); and a portrait of a priest (5).

1

2

3

4

5

6

7

8

9

Singapore's Chinese popula-tion accounted for 76 per cent of the total, or roughly 860,500 out of 1.12 million in the early 1950s. The demograp-hics of the community had changed dramatically. The 1931 census revealed that only 36 per cent of Singaporean Chinese were born in the Straits Settlements. The proportion had risen by 1947 to 60 per cent, and by the mid-1950s to 70 per cent. According to a 1947 social survey, more than half of the China-born immigrants had neither revisited China nor sent remittances to families there, so that the link with the motherland was more tenuous than was generally supposed. Indeed, the revelation of an unexpectedly large proportion of locally born Singaporeans in the 1947 census strengthened the argument for self-government.

The photographs here were snapped on the streets of Chinatown and include the portraits of its elderly female inhabitants (1 and 2) in the early 1960s; five-foot way occupants the letter writer (3) and fortune teller (4); preparations for the Festival of Lanterns (5) and praying for good fortune (6) in the early 1950s; a Chinese puppet theatre (7); and the interior of a death house in Sago Lane in 1960 (8).

1

2

3

4

5

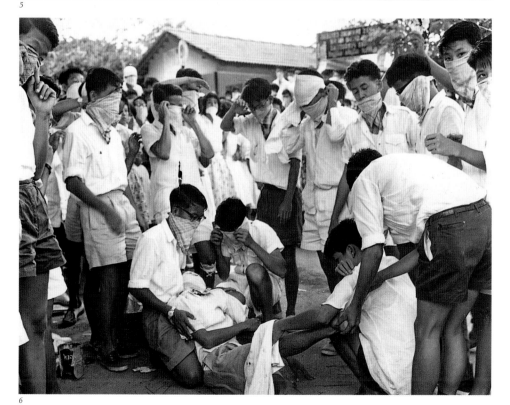

6

7

The volatile political activity of the 1950s was tinged with violence, giving rise to a new breed of photographer: the photojournalist.

Powerful images record the drama of the Maria Hertogh riots (1–3), as they are called, which erupted over a law suit contesting the custody of Maria Bertha Hertogh. Although the Dutch Catholic girl had been brought up by a Muslim family when her parents were interned by the Japanese, Maria's marriage to a Muslim was declared null and void, and her adoptive family ordered by court to return her to her natural parents. Till her return to Holland, she was placed in a Catholic Convent. On Monday 11 December 1950, the day that her foster mother, Che Aminah, was to have her appeal heard, a large Muslim crowd went berserk and began attacking Europeans and anyone who looked European. Two days of chaos ensued. At the end, 18 people were dead, 173 injured and 84 cars destroyed.

The 1956 Merdeka Rally (4) started peacefully. To rally public support for independence, David Marshall, as Chief Minister, had declared a Merdeka Week during which a mass signature campaign was launched. The week ended with a jubilant, gigantic all-party rally at old Kallang Airport. When the platform on which he stood collapsed, and he went down with it, violence erupted.

In May 1955, the Hock Lee bus strike (5) ended in violence in which two rioters, a student and an American correspondent, were killed. Many others were injured. The strike was politically motivated, involving a large number of Chinese school students and factory workers.

Various issues were used by extremists to stir up discontent among the Chinese-educated, of which the most notable was the proposed changes to Chinese middle school education (6) in 1961. Students held protests, boycotted examinations, picketed and blocked the Teachers' Training College and vandalized buses. Even the Ministry of Education came under siege.

Throughout the period from 1955 to 1959, the Communist United Front sought to discredit the Labour Front Government, and instigated the population through a series of confrontations. Strikes and work stoppages were common tactics (7). During these four years, there were 393 strikes and lock outs altogether. The worst year was 1955, with 275 strikes. Only a third were for better working conditions and wages; the others were either sympathy strikes or demands for the release of detained trade union leaders.

1 *Maria Hertogh riots, 1 December 1950. Che Aminah surrounded by supporters outside Supreme Court as riots break out after the court decides Maria must return to her Dutch parents who gave her up during the war.*
2 *The crowds outside Supreme Court*
3 *A car burns during the Maria Hertogh riots*
4 *Violence breaks out at the Merdeka Rally, Kallang, 18 March 1956*
5 *Hock Lee bus riots. Police erect barricades in Chinatown, 1955*
6 *Chinese student riots, November 1961*
7 *Strike action by Singapore Traction Company Employees Union, 1955*

1

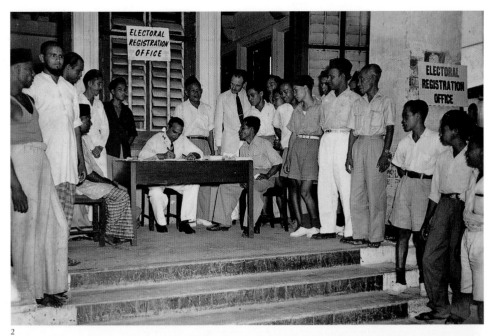

2

3

The road to nationhood—the two decades between the end of the Japanese Occupation in 1945 and the announcement of full independence on 9 August 1965—was marked by several milestones.

In 1946, Singapore became a Crown Colony while Penang and Malacca were absorbed into the Malayan Union. There were two reasons for this: firstly, Singapore was still important to Britain as a military base, and, secondly, Singapore's overwhelming Chinese population would have upset the racial balance in the Malay Peninsula. The need for some sort of political change was, however, recognized by the British. Singapore had its first ever elections in 1948 (2) when voters exercised their newly gained right to fill six seats of the Legislative Council. The pace of change accelerated with the acceptance of the Rendel Constitution in 1955. It paved the way for a popularly elected Legislative Assembly .

Among the newly formed parties was the People's Action Party (PAP) which was inaugurated on 21 November 1954. The meeting elected Toh Chin Chye as Chairman and Lee Kuan Yew as Secretary-General. The Labour Front emerged with moderate left-wing support. Its leader was a prominent lawyer and Iraqi Jew, David Marshall, then 47 years old.

The Rendel Constitution elections were held on 2 April 1955. Some 160,395 people voted. The Labour Front captured 10 seats and formed the first elected government of Singapore. David Marshall (6) became first Chief Minister.

1 Exercising the right to vote, City Council Elections, 1954
2 Voter registration, first Legislative Council elections, 1948. Voters had to be either British subjects or British-protected persons possessing property and holding certain residential status.
3 Arriving in style to vote, 1 April 1955
4 New Council Chambers undergoing renovation, 1 June 1954
5 Lim Yew Hock attends meeting of Rendel Constitution Commission, City Hall, 22 August 1954
6 Labour Party Leader and first Chief Minister of Singapore, David Marshall
7 Merdeka week referendum signing, 12 March 1956
8 Four parties' leaders meeting on 21 March 1956 including David Marshall and Lee Kuan Yew
9 PAP independence rally at Farrer Park on 15 August 1955. Seated are Lee Kuan Yew and (partially hidden) Lim Chin Siong.
10 The Rendel Constitution general elections and a victorious Lee Kuan Yew, the PAP candidate for Tanjong Pagar, carried by supporters, 2 April 1955

4

5

6

7

8

9

10

1

2

3

4

5

On 30 May 1959, Singapore's first general election for a fully elected government was held. More than half of the 587,797 voters were voting for the first time. The People's Action Party (PAP) scored a stunning victory, winning 43 of the 51 seats. The PAP had pledged that it would assume office only if the eight pro-communist PAP members detained in 1956 and 1957 were freed. Five days later, with huge crowds of supporters, the eight men were freed (7 and 8). In return, the detainees were asked to promise to work for a non-communist Malaya.

1 *Over a million leaflets and more than 150,000 posters in Malay, English, Chinese and Tamil urged voters to exercise their voting rights.*

2 *Lee Kuan Yew calls on Governor William Goode at Government House, 1 June 1959*

3 *PAP rally at Hong Lim Park*

4 *Election rally, Fullerton Square*

5 *Election day, 30 May 1959*

6 *PAP victory rally at City Hall steps, 3 June 1959*

7–8 *The release of the detainees (with garlands) from Changi Prison on 4 June 1959 was symbolized in the freeing of caged pigeons by Fong Swee Suan, S. Woodhull, Chan Chiaw Thor, Lim Chin Siong, Devan Nair and Tan Chong Kin.*

6

MERENTAH
RAKYAT
执政党人民

7

8

1

2

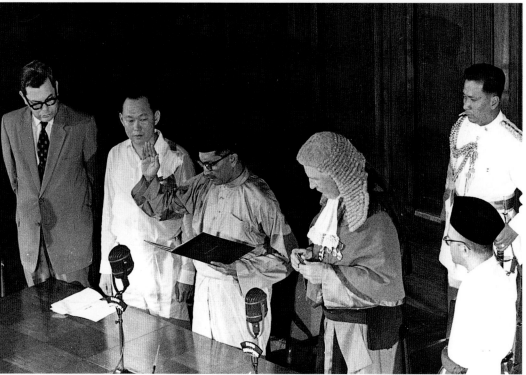

3

4

5

On 3 December 1959, Yusof bin Ishak was sworn in as the Yang di-Pertuan Negara (3). Soon after, Singapore's own flag, anthem and crest were introduced, and a National Loyalty Week launched (1).

Formidable obstacles faced the new government. The long years of colonial rule had cultivated in many people a subservience to—and dependence on—the colonial rulers. People's sense of belonging to Singapore was understandably weak. The priority was to instill a sense of unity and belonging amongst Singaporeans irrespective of ethnic origins. The English-educated, who had fared better than the others under colonial rule, had to be persuaded to share their privileges. The loyalty of the Chinese-educated needed to be won over. Malay, Chinese, Tamil and English were all made official languages, and used simultaneously in the Legislative Assembly (4).

1 *Rally at the Padang to celebrate the swearing in of Yusof bin Ishak as Yang di-Pertuan Negara and to launch National Loyalty Week, 3 December 1959*
2 *Flags along North Bridge Road during National Day, 3 June 1962*
3 *Swearing in of Yusof bin Ishak as Yang di-Pertuan Negara on 3 December 1959. Present are Sir George Oehlers, the Speaker of Parliament; Prime Minister Lee Kuan Yew; Chief Justice Sir Alan Rose; and Ahmad Ibrahim, the Attorney General.*
4 *Members of the Legislative Assembly, 1962*
5 *Dr Toh Chin Chye at a public lecture on how to fight colonialism, 1960*

These photographs from 1960 vividly capture a unique moment in Singapore's history when, quite literally, new brooms swept away the old. Thousands of Singaporeans led by ministers, assemblymen and People's Action Party supporters were mobilized to clean up the city. Signs were posted announcing the campaign (1). Prime Minister Lee Kuan Yew was photographed hosing down a street in Tanjong Pagar (2) where he also visited constituents during the Hong Lim by-election in 1961 (5). Already, plans were being made for an industrial centre in Jurong; Deputy Prime Minister Dr Goh Keng Swee was photographed viewing the site (4).

1 The clean up begins
2 Cleaning up Chinatown, 23 November 1959
3 Microphone in hand, Ong Eng Guan speaks to Chinatown residents
4 Deputy Prime Minister Dr Goh Keng Swee tours Jurong industrial
* site, 2 July 1960*
5 Lee Kuan Yew on house-to-house visits for Hong Lim by-election,
* 19 March 1961*

1

2

3

4

5

1

2

3

4

Fires periodically raged through squatter areas, but nowhere was as vulnerable as Bukit Ho Swee, one of the most crowded *attap* slums in Singapore. Named after Singapore-born pioneer Tay Ho Swee (1834–1903), it contained thousands of squatter huts made with combustible materials like attap and wood. There was no electricity or piped water. Here the poorest of the population—hawkers, secret society gangsters and the unemployed—found shelter. In 1934, more than 5,000 people lost their homes in a fire which spread rapidly through Bukit Ho Swee, Tiong Bahru and Havelock Road.

On 25 May 1961, a Hari Raya holiday, Bukit Ho Swee was the scene of the biggest ever fire in Singapore which carved out over 25 hectares of devastation and ruin. Some 22 fire engines arrived on the scene to battle the blaze. Two oil mills, three timber yards and three motor workshops were destroyed. Four people died and almost 3,000 families were made homeless.

The government organized food and shelter for victims. Army cooks fed victims housed in five schools in the Kim Seng Road area. It was announced that the government would acquire part of the land to build 12,000 low-cost flats for the homeless. By February 1962, all families affected by the fire were rehoused in Housing and Development Board flats.

The area was gradually transformed into a public housing estate. What remained of the squatters' village was destroyed in another fire seven years later, in 1968.

FACING PAGE **Balloting for new Housing and Development Board flats in Bukit Ho Swee Estate, 1962**
1 Kampong Tiong Bahru fire victims remove belongings, 15 February 1959
2–4 Scenes from the Bukit Ho Swee fire, 25 May 1961

1

Two of the most critical issues facing Singapore in the early 1960s were housing and jobs. The solution to the unemployment problem was large scale industrialization. Jurong, chosen to be the industrial heart of Singapore, was surveyed by a United Nations mission (1), which made recommendations on types of industries. By the end of 1963, nearly 730 hectares of land was ready for new factories. One of the major foreign investments of the time was the $30 million Shell Refinery on Pulau Bukom, which opened in July 1961 (3).

In 1960, a new statutory body, the Housing and Development Board (HDB), was created and entrusted with the challenge of housing Singaporeans. The urgency of meeting the housing need meant building large numbers of flats quickly and at minimum cost (6–10). At the end of its first five-year building programme, the HDB had completed 54,430 dwelling units.

The National Theatre (2) was built to mark the attainment of self-government. Citizens from all walks of life gave donations towards its building.

1 *Industrial survey team, led by Dr Goh Keng Swee, inspects industrial potential of Jurong swampland, 2 August 1960*
2 *National Theatre under construction. It opened in 1963 with a Southeast Asian cultural festival.*
3 *Shell Refinery, Pulau Bukom*
4 *Opening of Khong Guan Flour Mills on 31 March 1964*
5 *Dr Goh Keng Swee tours Bata's shoe factory at Telok Blangah, 9 April 1964*
6–7 *Semi-completed HDB flats at Alexandra, Tiong Bahru and Duchess Estates, 5 July 1960*
8 *Building works at St Michael's Housing Estate, c. 1962*
9 *Prime Minister Lee Kuan Yew tours building sites for public housing, 18 September 1959*
10 *Cambodia's King Sihanouk visits HDB estates, 19 December 1962*

2

3

4

5

6

7

8

9

10

1

2

3

4

5

8

It was a widely held assumption that Singapore could survive and prosper only if it was part of Malaysia, which had attained independence on 31 August 1957. The government of Malaysia, however, had discouraged merger with Singapore because it felt that the inclusion of a million Singaporean Chinese would upset the delicate racial balance in Malaya.

That thinking changed in 1961, after the People's Action Party's (PAP) leftist members broke away to form the Barisan Socialis (thus posing a threat to the moderates' majority in the Legislative Assembly), and when Ong Eng Guan with pro-communist support trounced moderate PAP candidate, Jek Yuen Thong, in a by-election. Malaysian Prime Minister Tunku Abdul Rahman became concerned about the growing power of the pro-communists. Discussions between the Tunku and Lee Kuan Yew ironed out the terms of Singapore's status within the Federation of Malaya. Yet on joining Malaysia on 16 September 1963, Singapore entered a stormy political period. The differences in the political and social systems led to friction. Soon, these differences manifested themselves in communal tensions which finally erupted into racial riots in Singapore on 21 July 1964. The whole island was put under curfew, but the disturbances continued for a week, during which 23 people were killed and 454 injured. To calm things down, Lee Kuan Yew (3) and Tunku Abdul Rahman (4) toured Singapore. However, lingering hostilities again led to communal violence in early September.

On 9 August 1965, Malaysia's parliament, the Dewan Rakyat, passed a bill approving separation for Singapore. At a televised press conference that afternoon Lee Kuan Yew announced the separation. He later recalled his emotions on that day: 'Every time we look back at the moment we signed this document it is for us a moment of anguish. For me it is a moment of anguish. All my life, my whole adult life, I have believed in merger and unity of the two territories. We are connected by geography, the economy and ties of kinship … It broke everything we stood for.'

1 *Malaysia Day celebrations at City Hall steps, 26 September 1963*
2 *Lee Kuan Yew visits the entire island to explain merger to the people*
3–4 *Lee Kuan Yew and Tunku Abdul Rahman tour in the aftermath of the 1964 communal riots to calm the public*
5 *Victory rally at Fullerton Square after an impressive PAP win in the polls*
6 *The curfew was lifted for a few hours daily to enable people to buy food and other necessities. Armed troops patrolled the streets to prevent any outbreak of violence.*
7 *Communal riots. By the time the curfew ended on 2 August 1964, 23 people were dead and 454 injured.*
8 *A tearful Lee Kuan Yew at the televised press conference during which he announced the separation agreement, 9 August 1965*

CHAPTER 5

ISLAND, CITY, STATE
1965–2000

The tears were shed, the press conference over, the news printed. Shock had given way to numbing recognition. From 9 August 1965, Singapore was on its own. The machinery of nationhood was quickly set in motion. Within days the country was declared a Republic and the Legislative Assembly rechristened Parliament. Malay was retained as the national language and English, Chinese and Tamil continued as official languages. International recognition was a priority, and on 21 September that year Singapore officially joined the United Nations as its 117th member. Yet many problems loomed—immediate, awesome and intimidating—and many sceptics wondered. How would trade expand? Where would new jobs come from? What about defence? Could Singapore survive?

And yet, by 1969—when the city was bedecked and bannered for the celebration of the 150th anniversary of Raffles' first landing at the Singapore River—Singapore was a politically stable state with a high rate of economic growth. The basic problems of survival had been overcome; the fundamentals were in place. When former Deputy Prime Minister Dr Goh Keng Swee reflected back on the 1960s, from the vantage point of the mid-1980s, he summed it up thus: 'Throughout the decade there was a persistent search for practical solutions, a patient building of institutions and infrastructure, a generous allocation of funds, an accumulation of talented staff. In the end it paid off.' Lee Kuan Yew's unequivocal answer to the question of what was the single most important factor for Singapore's rapid development since 1959 was the quality of its people. 'For not only are our people hardworking, quick to learn and practical, Singapore also had an extra thick layer of high calibre and trained talent.'

Among the other factors working in Singapore's favour was the economic buoyancy in the United States of America, Europe and Japan. Trade flourished and foreign entrepreneurs began to invest. Here to greet them were officers of the Economic Development Board (EDB). The Board was formed in 1961 on the advice of Dr Albert Winsemius, a Dutch economist who acted as a consultant to Singapore until his retirement in 1983. After a slow start, the EDB's work gained momentum. As a one-stop investment agency, it could assist in areas as diverse as financing and land clearing. Investors created much needed jobs and introduced Singapore to new technologies and new markets. The escalation of the Vietnam War also fuelled demand for goods and services.

The growing sense of security was given a jolt in 1968 with the unexpected news that the British were to relinquish their Singapore bases and accelerate their departure to 1971—four years earlier than expected. The British economy could no longer meet the financial demands of maintaining such a large presence east of Suez. The withdrawal meant the end of 40,000 jobs. Preparations began immediately so that when the last British vessel sailed away, the disruption was surprisingly minimal. The naval base at Sembawang was turned into a shipyard, while other bases were taken over by the Ministry of Defence or turned into industrial estates.

Meanwhile, the Housing and Development Board (HDB) was frantically building to rehouse the many squatters and slum dwellers living all over the island. In 1964, the Home Ownership Scheme was introduced, but its impact was only felt after 1968, when the government announced that savings accrued in Central Provident Fund accounts could be used to pay monthly mortgage instalments. Entire new towns appeared, housing between 250,000 and 300,000 residents, sometimes seemingly out of nowhere, in Queenstown, Toa Payoh, Ang Mo Kio, Bedok, Clementi and Jurong.

As developments multiplied in the 1970s, the need to give estates and new towns distinct identities became far more pressing. Given the constraints of high-rise, high-density housing, HDB experimented

ABOVE *Antique furniture, old street signs, discarded family photographs and architectural fragments. Singapore's past can be had—for a price.*
FACING PAGE *The ever-changing skyline, early 1990s. The dazzling financial district frames the partially restored shophouses of Chinatown.*

The MRT was the largest public works project in Singapore's history. The deepest of all stations, Raffles Place (left), was constructed in a densely built-up area. Work on Tanjong Pagar station (right) began in 1983 and was completed in 1987.

with colour, form and shape so that the uniform, regimentally placed blocks gave way to architecturally interesting, each with a full range of facilities and imbued with its own character and identity. Wherever possible, parks and green belts were carefully integrated to soften concrete edges.

The demand for flats continued unabated until the early 1990s because, as the housing needs of people eligible under the rules were met, the criteria for eligibility were further relaxed. Today, the client base includes everyone except the small percentage whose incomes enable them to pay the higher prices for private homes. The Board's goal has been refined to provide quality housing, in terms of size and finishes, to meet the demands of a more affluent and sophisticated population with rising aspirations. New estates include a greater mix of private and public housing, while mature estates are steadily being upgraded with better facilities and major refurbishment to existing blocks.

The HDB's resettlement programme released land in the central area for redevelopment, and, in 1966, an Urban Renewal Department was formed within the Board. Crucially, it was empowered to acquire land in the national interest. Smaller plots were thus assembled into larger ones for redevelopment. Between 1967 and 1969, 46 sites were released through the Sale of Sites Programme. The city turned into a patchwork of construction sites, the sky a tangle of building cranes. As the volume of work increased, and the land sales continued, a separate Urban Redevelopment Authority (URA) was formed as an independent statutory body in 1974.

In 1989, the URA was reorganized to incorporate a planning department. In doing so, its functions were expanded to include planning for future development and the management of development control. The Authority was also entrusted with the responsibility of conserving historically and culturally significant buildings and districts. As the conservation body, it laid the groundwork for the gazetting of unique areas, entire districts and many individual buildings, thereby ensuring the survival of over 5,000 mainly prewar shophouses. This triggered off the surge of restoration activity in the 1990s.

But perhaps it was the massive public works projects that have capped Singapore's transformation to global city: the expanded and modernized port facilities; the award-winning Changi International Airport; the system of expressways crossing the island; the cool, clean and convenient Mass Rapid Transit System (MRT); the land reclamation programme that has yielded space for a 21st century downtown; the network of hospitals delivering superb medical care; a diverse range of educational institutions, providing

Campaigns have played an important part in social development and public education, and have touched on issues as diverse as family planning and saving water. Among the most enduring are the Courtesy Campaign and the Speak Mandarin Campaign. Launched in 1979, they have become annual events.

HDB, NOL, SIA, CPF, DBS, EDB, TDB, URA, Like some secret code, the logos and acronyms of Singapore Inc.—here in placards at a 1990s National Day parade—bind a nation together.

the young with the best possible learning environment; and a world-class performing arts centre, Esplanade—Theatres on the Bay, scheduled to open in 2002.

Future historians might also point to the multitude of changes that have created a more cosmopolitan lifestyle: the shift from a manufacturing to a knowledge-based economy—or KBE—in which information and knowledge, rather than material resources, drive activities; the opening of the first Western fast-food restaurant (McDonalds, in 1979); the inaugural concert of the Singapore Symphony Orchestra, also in 1979; the growing sophistication of Orchard Road with the burgeoning of international designer shops in the 1980s; the growing respect for nature as seen in the creation of Sungei Buloh Nature Reserve; the establishment of a National Arts Council in 1991; the progress that women have made—as professionals, as Members of Parliament and in the Foreign Service; and, last but not least, the conquest of Mount Everest in May 1998. One other significant milestone was the handing over of leadership to a new generation. Although the People's Action Party has enjoyed three decades in power, it constantly regenerates itself with promising young leaders. On 28 November 1990, Goh Chok Tong was sworn in as Prime Minister, thus marking the end of one political era and the beginning of another. Another major change was the introduction of an elected President in 1993.

Pragmatic Singaporeans long ago learned to live with change. But feelings of nostalgia are often articulated in conversation. 'The house I lived in from the time I was six years old until I was 13 is gone; demolished for a highway,' wrote Simon Tay in 1991 in *Over Singapore*. 'The beach at Changi where my family went in the weekends of my youth has been reshaped by landfills and given over to the airport. The school I studied in has shifted to a

new building, in another part of the city. The field where I used to play football is now a car park … When returning to Singapore after five, three or even a single year, it is necessary to be prepared for new streets and buildings, a sense of displacement.' Journalist Monica Gwee, who moved back to Singapore in 1999 after a stint in Hong Kong, observed that the country had 'changed dramatically', not just physically 'but in countless small, precise and significant ways … Sometimes, home feels so much like a foreign country, I have to remind myself that it's all a mirage—really. The country has got itself a brand new hip wardrobe … and much international exposure, but really, deep down inside, maybe it's not that different from when I left it to live somewhere else.'

While the dramatic physical transformation is easy to capture in pictures, the intangibles are not. Yet, these have altered the island as surely as skyscrapers, new towns and expressways. The importance of people, of talent, continues to be a cornerstone. The ties that bind Singaporeans together are stronger now and embrace common experiences, ranging from education and National Service to a mutual passion for food and even a recognized brand of humour. Shared values have been promoted to encourage racial harmony and social stability. As Goh Chok Tong wrote in 1991 in the Foreword to *Singapore: The Next Lap*, 'The world is changing rapidly, but the basics remain the same. We have to make a living. Our most precious asset will always be our people. We must look after one another and build up our national spirit. Our security depends on our own efforts. Provided we are united and we anticipate our problems with ready solutions, whatever the future brings, we will be ready.' Nearly a decade later, the words still ring true. Tropical island, global city, prosperous multiracial nation state—modern Singapore is an epic work in progress.

Quest for the summit. The first Singaporean Mount Everest expedition team posed for team leader David Lim's camera at the Everest Base Camp, 1998. On 25 May 1998, two members of the team reached the highest peak in the world.

On 21 September 1965, Singapore was unanimously admitted to the United Nations as its 117th member. Lee Kuan Yew was determined to make this new nation a success. As a small country situated in a turbulent part of the world and dependent on trade and commerce for its survival, Singapore adopted a pragmatic foreign policy of friendship with as many countries as possible, irrespective of their ideology, so long as they did not engage in hostile acts against Singapore. By the time of the first National Day parade on 9 August 1966 (1), Singapore was gaining strength as an independent state.

1 *First National Day parade, 9 August 1966*
2 *Foreign Minister S. Rajaratnam (centre) with ASEAN counterparts, 1977*
3 *Visit of Chinese Senior Vice Premier Deng Xiaoping, 1978*
4 *Visit of Malaysian Prime Minister Tun Razak, 1973*
5 *Visit of Indian Prime Minister Indira Gandhi, 1968*
6 *Workers in Jurong welcome Crown Prince Akihito and his wife, 27 February 1970*
7 *Prime Minister Lee Kuan Yew and Deputy Prime Minister Dr Goh Keng Swee play golf with Burmese leader Ne Win, Island Club Bukit Course, 21 April 1968*
8 *Malaysian Prime Minister Datuk Hussein Onn leaves Singapore after a visit, 6 February 1976*

3

4

5

6

7

8

1

2

3

4

5

6

7

8

9

10

A multitude of events constituted nation-building in the late 1960s and 1970s: the campaigns, from Use Your Hands (1) to Tree Planting (2); activities held at community centres (8) and constituencies (9); the official visits of heads of state and foreign dignitaries (previous pages); the beginnings of National Service; special exhibitions, such as Police Week (3); balloting for Housing and Development Board flats; and the opening of a host of infrastructure projects ranging from factories (following pages) and educational institutions to mosques (10).

1 *The Use Your Hands Campaign. Prime Minister Lee Kuan Yew at Delta Circus Primary School, 6 June 1976*

2 *The Prime Minister celebrates Tree Planting Day, Marina Park, November 1976*

3 *Opening of Police Week by Minister for Home Affairs Prof. Wong Lin Ken, June 1972*

4 *Minister for Law E. W. Barker attends the opening of the Serangoon Gardens Hawker Centre, 1972*

5 *Senior Minister of State Goh Chok Tong at the Kite Flying Competition, East Coast Park, September 1978*

6 *Minister for Social Affairs Encik Othman Wok attends a picnic for the charges of social welfare homes at Pasir Ris, November 1969*

7 *Chan Chee Seng receives, as a donation, a day's earnings from the Singapore Trishaw Riders' Association for the National Relief Fund, April 1968*

8 *Foreign Minister S. Rajaratnam distributes Hari Raya gifts, Kampong Glam, September 1978*

9 *Minister for Finance Hon Sui Sen visits Ellenborough Market, September 1978*

10 *Encik Othman Wok at a ceremony to mark the sinking of the first pile for Jurong Mosque, 1977*

It was a modest beginning. On 17 July 1967, some 900 young men assembled at 'sending-off points' all over the island (1 and 2). Waiting to receive them at Taman Jurong Camp were 117 newly qualified officer cadets who had just graduated from the Singapore Armed Forces Training Institute (SAFTI) (8), having trained under battle-hardened Israeli advisors.

Interviewing those first recruits years later, Mickey Chiang recounted in *SAF and Thirty Years of National Service*: 'What [was] most remembered was the toughness of the training, the lack of privacy. They remember the darkened night when all lights in the camp were switched off except for little oil lamps around the parade square. A solemn atmosphere lay under the stars. As the name of each recruit was read out, he marched up and carefully received his "wife" whom he was told to take the best care of and to protect at all times. The "wife" was … his AR15 (or M16) assault rifle, on which his life now depended.'

Singapore's armed forces were created virtually from scratch. The government realized that, given a small population and the need for civilian manpower, it would be too costly to maintain a large standing army; defence would be based upon a citizen's army backed by trained reserves. Compulsory national service for all young Singaporean men would also help in nation building. In March 1967, the National Service Amendment Bill was passed, making registration for national service compulsory for all males who had reached the age of 18.

When national service started, the government assumed that it had eight to 10 years to develop a military capability before the British withdrawal. However, the early pull out of the British was a catalyst for the build up of Singapore's armed forces. On 31 October 1971, the last British military vessel steamed past Minister for Defence Dr Goh Keng Swee on its way home (6).

1 Send-off party for National Servicemen at MacPherson Community Centre, 19 January 1977

2 National Service registration, 28 March 1967

3 Reporting for duty at Central Manpower Base, 26 December 1967

4 Queen Elizabeth reviews the troops during her 1972 visit

5 Deputy Prime Minister and Minister for Defence Dr Goh Keng Swee attends the Singapore Armed Forces Display, Changi Air Base, 20 June 1975

6 The last British military vessel steams past Dr Goh on its way out of Singapore, 31 October 1971

7 A Royal Singapore Air Force pilot, Seletar Air Base, 6 October 1969

8 SAFTI, 1971

9 Hoisting of the Singapore Navy flag at Telok Ayer Basin, 5 May 1967

10 The handover of Seletar Air Base, 16 April 1969

5

6

7

8

9

10

By the time the Housing and Development Board (HDB) was formed on 1 February 1960, the need to improve the housing situation was exceedingly urgent: over half a million people living either in badly degenerated slums (1–4) or squatter areas needed rehousing. It did not, of course, happen overnight. Even as the HDB was placed under the Ministry of National Development (MND) in 1975, and housed in the new MND building overlooking Telok Ayer Street (5), there was a substantial waiting list for new flats.

No other country has gone so far with the social experiment of high-rise, high-density housing. One important turning point was the start of the Home Ownership Scheme in 1964, giving Singaporeans the opportunity to own their own homes. The low interest rates, coupled with the privilege, from 1968, of using one's Central Provident Fund savings as down payment and monthly instalments, made the scheme very successful. More importantly, it fostered a sense of belonging to the young nation. By the end of 1970, the HDB had completed more than 120,000 units and housed about 35 per cent of the population. Prices then ranged from $3,300 for a one-room (improved) flat to $12,500 for a four-room flat.

The turning point for the HDB, from being a flat builder to a new town developer, was around 1977 when the waiting list for housing had declined and the Board began to pay more attention to qualitative improvements. By the time the HDB celebrated its 25th anniversary in 1985, eight out of every 10 Singaporeans called a HDB flat home. Some 500,000 units had been built in dozens of estates and 10 new towns, where the amenities included markets and supermarkets, hawker centres, parks and car parks, childcare centres, neighbourhood police posts, playgrounds and swimming and sports complexes.

Toa Payoh (8), conceived in 1965, was the first new town to have a town centre and a range of facilities to complement housing. Towards the end of the 1970s, six new towns were started in quick succession: Yishun, Hougang, Jurong East and West, Tampines and Bukit Batok.

---

1 Sleeping accommodation, the slums of Chinatown, 1969
2 First floor, No. 29 Banda Street, 1969
3 Kitchen quarters, Chinatown, 1969
4 Sago Lane, 1969
5 Telok Ayer Street and the Ministry of National Development, 1970
6 HDB flats under construction on the edge of Chinatown, late 1960s
7 Balloting sessions for sale of flats at Queenstown, 1969
8 Sale of flats at Toa Payoh, the first satellite new town, 1966

6

7

8

1

2

By the early 1970s, most of the basic problems of survival had been overcome. Every day seemed to bring the opening of a new factory, a new school, the start of a new campaign, or the unveiling of a new project to improve the lives—and livelihoods—of Singaporeans and help plug the country into the global economy.

To curb the rapid population growth, the government set up the Singapore Family Planning and Population Board (5). The combination of incentives and disincentives, coupled with advice on family planning and contraception, worked well: from 1965 to 1970 the birth rate decreased significantly.

Post-independence, industrialization efforts were intensified. The Economic Development Board (EDB), set up in 1961, was reorganized in 1968 to concentrate on investment promotion. That year also saw the formation of both the Jurong Town Corporation and the Development Bank of Singapore. Industrial peace, together with investment promotion and supporting operations, caused an influx of foreign investors.

1 *Minister for Education Ong Pang Boon at the opening of the Nanyang University Computer Centre, 3 November 1969*
2 *Prime Minister Lee Kuan Yew and Mrs Lee at the opening of TV Singapura's new building, Caldecott Hill, 26 August 1966*
3 *Minister for Science and Technology Dr Toh Chin Chye briefs President Sheares on a scale model of the University of Singapore's new Kent Ridge campus, April 1971*
4 *President Sheares at the opening of the Sentosa Earth Satellite Station, 23 October 1971*
5 *Minister for Education Dr Lee Chiaw Meng attends a family planning seminar for teachers, 1975*
6 *Minister for Finance Lim Kim Sam tours pioneering industries at Jurong Industrial Estate, May 1967*
7 *Minister for Social Affairs Encik Othman Wok visits Roxy Electric Industries, Tanglin Halt Close, 1971*
8 *Opening of Texas Instruments factory, July 1969*
9 *At the opening of the 150 Years of Development exhibition, Dr Goh Keng Swee called for urgent action to shore up tottering buildings in the city centre until the urban renewal programme could get to them, August 1969*

3

6

7

4

8

5

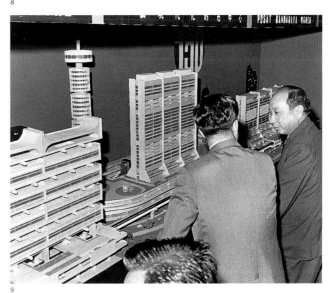

9

Miniskirts, long hair, drive-in movies, 'Instant Asia', football fever, a new zoo—and new educational opportunities. Singapore was changing rapidly and a generation of young people with it. The education system was pumped up and fine tuned. By 1965, nationwide free primary education had been implemented and, the following year, the teaching of a second language was made compulsory. The focus then shifted to secondary and tertiary education. As planning got underway for the new university campus at Kent Ridge (see page 334) as well as for improved technical education, Singapore's first junior college opened. In 1969, National Junior College (5) welcomed high-calibre students from both English- and Chinese-medium schools who were hand-picked for intensive pre-university training. Its success led to a mushrooming of well-equipped government-aided junior colleges in the 1970s and early 1980s.

1 *The Bambinos, winners of the 1954 Talentime, back on TV in 1965*
2 *Participants in the Miss Efficiency Contest, 1968*
3 *Trading on the Stock Exchange, 1966*
4 *A visit to the Istana calls for a snapshot, 1971*
5 *Students of the newly opened National Junior College welcome VIP visitor Princess Anne, 1972*
6 *President's Scholars pose with President Sheares at the Istana, July 1975*
7 *Opening ceremony of the 7th SEA (Southeast Asian) Games, Kallang Stadium, 1 September 1973*
8 *The drive-in cinema, Yuan Ching Road, Jurong, 1971*
9 *Dr Goh Keng Swee feeds the elephants at the official opening of thr Singapore Zoological Gardens, 27 June 1973*
10 *'Instant Asia'. Singapore's early tourism campaign*
11 *Football history comes to Singapore. Brazilian legend Pele obliges fans during his 1974 visit.*

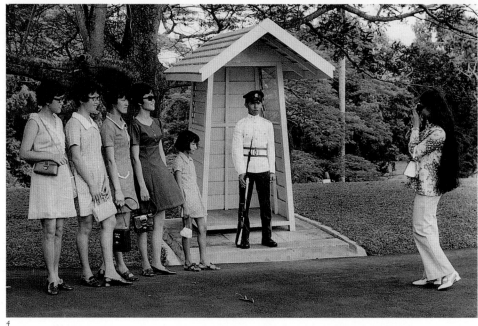

5

8

9

6

10

7

11

1

2

3

4

5

6

7

8

9

10

11

The Sixties saw the birth of the local English popular music scene which continued to flourish in the Seventies. The hugely popular Cliff Richard (5) spawned a generation of imitators, and the Rolling Stones came to town (2). Milestones of the Seventies included the 1972 launch of Singapore Airlines and the Singapore Girl (3), the 1973 opening of Kallang Stadium (11) and the rise of the 'Kallang Roar', and the 1979 inaugural concert of the Singapore Symphony Orchestra (9).

1 *Matthew and the Mandarins, 1978*
2 *The Rolling Stones in Singapore, February 1965*
3 *Singapore Airlines and the Singapore Girl were introduced in 1972*
4 *Finalists of Singapore's 150th Anniversary Beauty Contest, 1969*
5 *Cliff Richard and fans, April 1973*
6 *Promoting acceptable hairstyles during the Anti-Long Hair Campaign, September 1974*
7 *The top three winners of the Kebaya Contest, Gay World Stadium, 1968*
8 *Family act: Pat and Mark Chan performing together, October 1978*
9 *Singapore Symphony Orchestra's inaugural concert under the baton of Maestro Choo Huey, January 1979*
10 *Go-kart racing, 1970*
11 *Soccer star Dollah Kassim congratulated by team-mates, 19 August 1979*

FOLLOWING PAGES
Singapore from the air. The seafront and downtown skyline on the brink of redevelopment, c. 1965

By the time Singapore celebrated its 150th anniversary in 1969, the entire central area of Singapore (preceding pages) was ripe for development. Urban redevelopment officially began in 1966, when the Urban Renewal Department was formed as part of the Housing and Development Board. Empowered to acquire land in the national interest, it prepared a master plan for redevelopment, and then embarked on an ambitious programme to clear slums, rehouse people and improve the infrastructure of the city. Between 1967 and 1969, 46 sites were released through the Sale of Sites Programme. The cranes were flying—and a new financial district was in the making, enabling Singapore to take on the role of a regional financial hub. In 1974, the separate Urban Redevelopment Authority was formed.

1 *A flurry of construction at the junction of Cantonment Road and Anson Road, 1980. All photographs by Chu Sui Miong, who for many years ran Fee Fee House of Photographics in Hong Lim Complex. From a collection donated to the National Archives of Singapore by his family.*
2 *Shenton Way, c. 1970*
3 *The new downtown landscape. Shenton Way and the Development Bank of Singapore Tower, 1970s*
4 *River Valley Road with Liang Court under construction, 1980*
5 *Singapore celebrates its 150th anniversary, Collyer Quay, 1969*
6 *North Bridge Road, 1970*
7 *Where Orchard Road meets Dhoby Ghaut, c. 1970*

3

5

6

4

7

1

2

3

Orchard Road (1) has changed beyond recognition since this photograph was taken by S. M. Chu around 1970—about the same time that a high-rise skyline began to frame the shophouses of Boat Quay (2); Housing and Development Board flats were rising on the island's northern shore (7); and the National Stadium, completed in 1973 (5), was being built.

Although Changi was a major candidate for the site of a new commercial airport from as early as 1946, it was not until the mid-1970s that advances in soil treatment, consolidation, engineering and mechanical construction made it practicable. The decision to use the site was made in 1975, and Changi International Airport opened on 1 July 1981. The project involved massive land reclamation with every square metre consolidated for stability. One of the more spectacular feats was the winching of the 1350-tonne control tower cabin into position (4).

Work on the Mass Rapid Transit System (MRT) began in 1983. On 11 November 1987, the first train pulled out of Bishan depot to pick up passengers. Three weeks later, the millionth ride was recorded. Fast, clean, cool and convenient, the MRT changed the face of the island (6).

---

1 *Orchard Road looking north towards the junction with Scotts Road. The Hilton Hotel is under construction, 1960s.*
2 *Construction begins to change the skyline by the Singapore River, 1970*
3 *South Bridge Road with South Bridge Centre under construction and, in the distance, Raffles City taking shape, 1980*
4 *Changi Airport control tower under construction, early 1980s*
5 *National Stadium (left) and Kallang Indoor Stadium (right) under construction, March 1973*
6 *Ang Mo Kio MRT station, 1980s*
7 *Woodlands New Town under construction, 1970s*

1

2

3

4

5

6

7

8

9

10

The contrast between the modern city and an older, but fast disappearing, way of life captivated both Singaporean and foreign photographers, who from the 1970s focused their cameras on all manner of scenes to produce images for an increasing number of illustrated books. Their work ranged from the artistic and picturesque to sharply rendered scenes of human vulnerability. Albert Lim's interior of a Hastings Road coffee shop (5) was reproduced in *Singapore: Island, City, State* which was published in 1990 to celebrate a quarter century of nationhood. It followed upon the landmark *Salute to Singapore*, published in 1984 to celebrate 25 years of self-rule, which brought together 41 of the world's leading photographers.

1 **Samsui** *women, elderly but still active*
2–3 *Chinatown's street traffic*
4 *Singaporeans of all races have acquired a taste for the durian*
5 *Coffee shop on Hastings Road*
6 *Unlicensed street hawkers*
7–8 *Life in the last remaining kampongs*
9 *Chinese junks and city skyline*
10 *Sweat and sheer hard labour still moved goods in the 1970s*

1

2

Just as the early artists positioned themselves in boats near the shore, contemporary photographers have availed themselves of helicopters to capture the view of Singapore from the sea (above). The transformation of the financial district was an important milestone in the process of redevelopment. Raffles Institution was still near the shoreline in the 1970s (2), but within a few years the area was reclaimed as Marina Central, and, at the school site, Raffles City was under construction (3).

A strange hush fell over the Singapore River (1) in September 1983 when several hundred lighters made their final journey out to the open sea to their new anchorage at Pasir Panjang (see page 350). Although the sight saddened many, it was predicted that the lighter industry would have died a natural death as, with containerization and improved port facilities, the boats were no longer needed.

ABOVE From the sea: a new financial centre takes shape, fronted by the land reclamation at Marina South and Marina Central, mid-1970s
1 Bumboats on the River, c. 1980
2 From the air: Raffles Institution and the Civilian War Memorial
3 Megaprojects underway: the construction of Raffles City and Marina Square

3

'The approach to Singapore by air is majestic, but no one has seen Singapore who has not spent several hours on the harbour, going between the ships and the islands and at the same time always aware of the huge presence of the city,' wrote Geoffrey Dutton in 1981 in *Impressions of Singapore*.

Singapore is the busiest port in the world in terms of shipping tonnage. Ships of more than 400 shipping lines fly flags of virtually all the maritime countries, linking Singapore to about 700 ports. In the 1990s, the former Port of Singapore Authority (PSA) was restructured into two organizations: PSA Corporation, the world's largest container terminal operator, and the Maritime and Port Authority of Singapore (MPA), a statutory board formed in 1996 and the sole regulatory body responsible for port and maritime affairs.

In 1998, PSA Corporation handled almost 15 million TEUs (20-foot equivalent units). Ships berth at one of four container terminals: Tanjong Pagar, Keppel, Brani and Pasir Panjang. The ultramodern megacontainer terminal at Pasir Panjang has been built to meet the demands of the future. Phase I of the $7 billion project serviced its first ships in 1998 with state-of-the-art equipment, including the world's first remote controlled yard cranes which allow containers to be stacked nine levels high.

1 The Tanjong Pagar Container Terminal is separated from the city by the thin line of an expressway
2 Bumboat anchorage in Pasir Panjang, early 1990s
3 Oil rigs in the harbour, c. 1993
4 The old Clifford Pier overlooks the new Marina Bay
5–7 Port and city continue to evolve in tandem with each other. At any one time, there are more than 800 ships calling at Singapore.

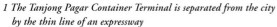

5

6

7

'Cities are constantly changing and so are the visions that shape them,' wrote Chua Beng Huat in 1989 in *The Golden Shoe: Building Singapore's Financial District*. 'Only three decades ago it was the urgent need for urban renewal which guided Singapore's planners. Today the goal is no less ambitious than to transform Singapore into an elegant tropical city, the first developed city in the equatorial belt and one of the great cities of the world in the next century.' At the end of the 20th century, the transition is well underway.

Raffles Place (facing page) has seen many changes since its formation in the 1820s. It is now a park framed by the two entrances to the Raffles Place MRT station. The new downtown skyline includes buildings designed by world famous architects such as I. M. Pei, Kenzo Tange, Philip Johnson, Helmut Jahn, Kevin Roche and Paul Rudolph. The reclaimed land of Marina Centre (2) supports three megaprojects: the convention centre, office and shopping complex Suntec City, Marina Square and Millennium Walk.

FACING PAGE *Raffles Place, 1999*
1 *Bird's eye view of downtown skyscrapers along Collyer Quay and Raffles Place*
2 *The trio of developments at Marina Bay: Marina Square, Suntec City and Millennium Walk, early 1990s*

The abacus has given way to the credit card, and the smells of petrol, sweat and garbage have succumbed to the aroma of freshly brewed coffee, but the entrepreneurial spirit still remains. After the bumboats left in 1983, Boat Quay stood forlorn until the entire area was gazetted for conservation in 1989. By the early 1990s, nearly all the shophouses once occupied by the old Chinese trading companies were in the throes of reconstruction.

Today, pubs and restaurants line the elegantly paved river bank (1 and 3), where customers dine against a historical backdrop. Further upriver is Clarke Quay (2). The former warehouse district contains more than 50 restored shophouses and godowns, and opened as a Festival Village in 1993. Here, bumboats are permanently docked, in service as restaurants.

BELOW Looking its best: Boat Quay at dusk, 1990s
1 The restored shophouses of Boat Quay
2 At Clarke Quay Festival Village, bumboats are used for outdoor dining.
3 Alfresco dining at Boat Quay

1

2

3

1

2

3

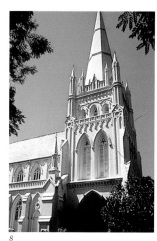

4

9

At the heart of the civic district is the Padang (1), around which are the well-weathered stones of empire, from the stately Supreme Court (2 and 3) to the colonial buildings revitalized as museums. The Singapore History Museum (4 and 7) focuses on Singapore's political and social history. The Singapore Art Museum (6 and 9) officially opened in January 1996, and houses one of the world's largest collection of contemporary Southeast Asian art. The Asian Civilizations Museum (5), opened in April 1997, traces Singapore's multiethnic heritage by focusing on the art and artefacts of Southeast, East, West and South Asia.

1 Flag over the Padang, National Day celebrations, early 1980s
2 The Allegory of Justice, Supreme Court
3 The signature dome of Supreme Court and the rarely seen smaller one
4 and 7 The Singapore History Museum occupies the old Raffles
    Library and Museum
5 Interior of the Asian Civilizations Museum, housed in the former
    Tao Nan School
6 and 9 The Singapore Art Museum is the former St Joseph's Institution
8 The spire of St Andrew's Cathedral remains a familiar landmark

FOLLOWING PAGES
Private and public, the Singapore River divides the low-rise colonial
buildings from the skyscrapers which today define the financial district.

5

1

2

3

4

The move to conserve the city's historical fabric culminated in the unveiling of a visionary Conservation Master Plan in 1987 which nominated for preservation and conservation several large areas and more than 3,000 buildings 'in order to safeguard them for future Singaporeans'.

At the heart of the plan are three main districts: Chinatown, Kampong Glam and Little India. Chinatown, the largest, covers Telok Ayer, Kreta Ayer, Bukit Pasoh and Tanjong Pagar (1). Kampong Glam (5), like a small village in a great city, contains 620 conservation buildings and the Istana Kampong Glam which was built in the 1840s as the home of Sultan Hussein and is earmarked to become the Malay Heritage Centre. Little India (6–8) has about 900 conservation buildings, and was once aptly described by a local restaurant proprietor as an 'every kind of people coming place'.

1 The rooftops of Tanjong Pagar, one of four areas in the Chinatown
  conservation district
2–3 Restored buildings on Duxton Hill
4 Nos. 15–17 Trengganu Street
5 The Kampong Glam conservation district, early 1990s
6–8 Scenes from Little India, 1999

1

2

3

4

5

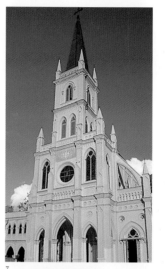

6

7

8

9

10

11

12

13

14

15

Since its founding in 1971, the Preservation of Monuments Board has gazetted 43 structures, buildings and statues as National Monuments. These include important religious buildings—Chinese and Indian temples, mosques and churches—as well as former colonial institutions and significant urban landmarks. Among those restored in the 1980s and 1990s were Telok Ayer Market (4), Raffles Hotel (6) and the former Convent of the Holy Infant Jesus, now Chijmes (7).

1 *Alkaff Mansion. A restored family home is now a restaurant and an events venue.*
2 *The* gopuram, *or tower, of Sri Mariamman Temple*
3 *The Alsagoff School, or Madrasah, in Kampong Glam*
4 *A clock tower crowns Telok Ayer Market*
5 *Thian Hock Kheng temple remains a Chinatown landmark*
6 *The restored Raffles Hotel opened its doors in 1991*
7 *Chijmes Hall, the former chapel of the Convent of the Holy Infant Jesus*
8 *Dalhousie Obelisk, Empress Place*
9 *Former Hill Street Police Station, after restoration and conversion to the Ministry of Information and the Arts*
10 *Goodwood Park Hotel was built as the Teutonia Club in the 1890s*
11 *The Cathedral of the Good Shepherd*
12 *Tan Kim Seng Fountain, Esplanade Park*
13 *Steps of the Cenotaph, Esplanade Park*
14 *City Hall is dramatically lit at night*
15 *Old Parliament House. The last sitting was in September 1999.*

1

Prewar residential terraces have become sought after as homes in areas such as Blair Road, once a strongly Peranakan neighbourhood; Joo Chiat and Koon Seng Roads (13), where 504 shophouses were gazetted for conservation in 1993; and Emerald Hill, with its unique environment and close proximity to Orchard Road. Most of the terraces were built during the suburban boom years, between the early 1900s and the early 1930s, and are instantly recognizable because of their characteristic facades—an elaborate and eclectic mixture of Chinese, Malay, European and colonial architectural elements.

No. 41 Emerald Hill Road (1–4) is one of a trio of unusual three-storey houses designed in 1905 by G. A. Fernandez and Co. for Goh Kee Hoon. The original building plans were signed by Wan Mohamed Kassim. The house was in an extremely dilapidated state when it was acquired in 1989 by Dr and Mrs M. C. Tong, but underneath the grime many of the architectural details were still intact, and the entire building was carefully restored as a family home. At the heart of the house is an airwell (4), featuring intricate plasterwork decoration on the walls and a carp pond (2).

3

1 *Front door and half door, or* pintu pager, *of No. 41 Emerald Hill Road. This and the other photographs on the page were taken in 1994.*
2 *Directly above the pond is an open-to-the-sky airwell*
3 *The second floor study and music room overlook Emerald Hill Road*
4 *The area around the airwell was used as a family room*
5–13 *Among the characteristics of the classic terraces are the three bays of windows on the upper storey, Malay fretwork eaves, flat columns known as pilasters, ornate plasterwork decoration and pastel colours.*

2

4

5

6

8

7

9

10

11

12

13

Orchard Road is Singapore's glamour street and a symbol of the good life. But what was once 'a well-shaded avenue to an English mansion' (see pages 128–9) is now a thoroughly modern boulevard lined with a string of shopping malls (1–4) and hotels. Most of the city lives on Orchard Road, or so it sometimes seems on weekends when the shaded pedestrian walkways bubble over with irrepressible energy. Landmarks at the junction with Scotts and Paterson Roads (below) include C. K. Tang, on the right, and Shaw Building, on the site of the old Lido Cinema (see page 273) which lives on in the well-patronized cineplex upstairs.

BELOW Singapore's most cosmopolitan junction: where Orchard Road meets Scotts Road
1 Paragon is one of several older malls that have been given a glamorous update at the end of the 1990s
2 Modern landmarks: Wisma Atria, the twin towers of Ngee Ann City and the Mandarin Hotel
3 The glass pyramid of Wheelock Place is a popular meeting point
4 The Heeren Building is the second so-called on the site; it replaced a 1930s building that was in its day the talk of the town.

1

2

3

4

1

2

3

4

5

6

7

8

9

10

The city has many facets—too numerous to sum up in the pages of any book, facets which change in response to the flow of technology, new ideas, new products, new places and a new generation of Singaporeans who are ever quick to plug into global culture. Cybercafés (1), air-conditioned food courts (2), shopping atriums (7 and 11), cultural and family events on Fort Canning (6) and dining alfresco (5) are only some likely to be remembered when the 20th century is looked back upon.

1 *Cybercafé*
2 *Air-conditioned food courts are found throughout the city*
3 *Orchard Road skateboarder*
4 *Coffee culture*
5 *Dining alfresco at Peranakan Place, Emerald Hill*
6 *Picnic in the park, Fort Canning*
7 *Innovative architecture: shophouse facades face indoors at Bugis Junction*
8 *Books and browsers at Borders bookshop*
9 *Strolling along shady Orchard Road*
10 *The ubiquitous taxi*
11 *One of the biggest atriums is in the I. M. Pei-designed Raffles City*
12 *Downtown is only an MRT ride away*

It all began with the Tree Planting Campaign in 1963. Since then, the ongoing planting of trees and other plants, the creation of new green spaces and public parks and the careful conservation of older ones, have enhanced the urban environment and softened harsh edges. Everyone has his or her favourite green corner of the city, whether it be a park, a tree-lined avenue such as Nassim Road (6), or something more spectacular, like the gardens of the Shangri-La Hotel's garden wing (11).

The city's two most historical parks have been well integrated into the civic district. Fort Canning (4)—the 19-hectare 'hill of history'—is now also a premier venue for cultural activities. Esplanade Park is home to several historical monuments including the memorial (3) to World War II hero Lim Bo Seng.

The distinguished history of the Singapore Botanic Gardens (12–14) is embedded in its flora. Since 1859, it has not only provided beauty and pleasure to generations but is well known as a scientific institution. Among its treasures is one of the last vestiges of the island's original vegetation: 4 hectares of virgin native jungle. Efforts are being made to conserve as much of it as possible, in spite of the difficulties in maintaining the ecological balance in so small a tract.

Spacious old bungalows are a relatively rare commodity. Some have survived as embassies and ambassadorial residences, such as Eden Hall (7), home of the British High Commissioner. Black-and-white houses (9) were built as quarters for senior British civil servants and are an adaptive eclectic cross between a Malay kampong house and English domestic architecture.

1 Orchid gardens in Mandai
2 Still life on pond
3 Esplanade Park and the Lim Bo Seng Memorial
4 Ancient trees and remnants of the old Christian cemetery on Fort Canning
5 Duxton Plain Park, early 1990s
6 Nassim Road
7 Eden Hall, residence of the British High Commissioner, Nassim Road
8 Shell House
9 A classic black-and-white bungalow
10 French Embassy, Gallop Road
11 Garden wing of the Shangri-La Hotel
12–14 The Singapore Botanic Gardens

6

11

12

13

7

8

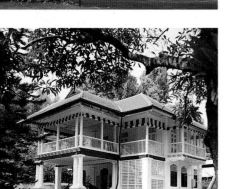

9

10

14

1

2

3

Today, the HDB's goal is to provide quality housing to meet the demands of a more affluent and sophisticated population with rising aspirations. In 1993, the World Habitat Award for the best-planned new town in the world was bestowed on Tampines New Town. The HDB vocabulary is peppered with new terms such as 'Punggol 21' (the master plan for a new HDB towns with innovative planning concepts and novel design features); 'Design Plus' (upmarket flats designed by HDB architects to provide greater variety); and 'Design-and-Build Flats' (designed by private architects and engineers in partnership with contractors). At the same time, mature estates are being upgraded with new facilities and major facelifts.

But beyond architecture, the HDB has played a key role in nation building. Housing policies have supported the institution of the family and encouraged ethnic integration. By the end of 1998, the HDB had built 861,974 flats to house nine out of every 10 Singaporeans. More significantly, over 81 per cent of HDB heartlanders are flat owners.

1 *View from above. Older blocks dominate downtown areas such as Rochor and Serangoon as well as areas beyond.*
2 *HDB of the 1970s: typical retangular blocks at Telok Blangah*
3 *HDB of the 1990s: new style blocks in Woodlands*
4 *Point blocks at Jurong East*
5 *New generation HDB. Design-and-build flats at Bukit Batok*
6 *Bishan New Town. The impact of high-rise, high-density housing is cushioned by parks.*
7 *Suburban Singapore: brick buildings and MRT at Hougang*
8 *Clothes on bamboo poles flutter like so many flags in the wind*

1

2

3

4

Pockets of near-wilderness are almost startling in an island of only 648 square kilometres and a population of over 3.8 million. Yet they do exist. The National Parks Board manages about 2796 hectares of nature reserves, including the Bukit Timah Nature Reserve (6) which was established in 1883. It also looks after about 500 hectares of mangrove forest along the northern shore and the Sungei Buloh Nature Park (7), home to some 160 species of birds, including migratory birds from as far away as Siberia. The Board's portfolio also covers more than 952 hectares of parks and open spaces and over 4000 hectares of roadside greenery, including the famous hanging bougainvillea (1).

Recreational land within the reservoir areas—MacRitchie, Pierce and Seletar (3 and 5)—is managed by the Public Utilities Board. Jurong Bird Park (8) is home to over 8,000 birds representing 600 species from around the world, including some endangered species. The Singapore Zoological Gardens is located by Seletar Reservoir (2) and is one of the few open zoos in the world, where animals roam freely in specially landscaped enclosures designed to recreate their natural habitats. Covering 28 hectares, the park houses close to 3,000 animals representing 250 species of mammals, reptiles and birds.

1 *Bougainvillea softens an expressway*
2 *Little Guilin, a lake in Bukit Batok Town Park*
3 *Seletar Reservoir*
4 *Bukit Timah Nature Reserve*
5 *Singapore Zoological Gardens*
6 *The view from Bukit Timah Hill, Bukit Timah Nature Reserve*
7 *Bird sanctuary, Sungei Buloh Nature Reserve*
8 *Jurong Bird Park*

5

6

7

8

As a small state, Singapore must be prepared to defend itself. Today, every Singaporean participates in 'Total Defence'. This embraces five components: Economic, Psychological, Military, Social and Civil Defence. Among young men, national service (2–5) remains a significant rite of passage.

In health and education, the advances have been enormous. The island is served by 21 hospitals, of which eight are government run and the remaining 13 private. In 1998, there were, in addition, 1,676 private clinics and 17 polyclinics. Amongst the newest hospitals is KK Women's and Children's Hospital (11) which specializes in obstetrics, gynaecology and pediatrics.

Every young Singaporean has the opportunity to enjoy at least 10 years of good basic education, and the trend is to continue studies in junior colleges, polytechnics or vocational institutes. At the end of 1998, there were a total of 188 primary schools and 142 secondary schools, including the oldest, Raffles Institution (10), 5 full schools and 14 junior colleges. The bilingual policy ensures that pupils learn English and their mother tongue. Singaporeans have been quick to respond to information technology, and computers are a part of daily life (14).

1 *Commando training*
2–5 *Scenes of National Service, 1999*
6 *Singapore Airlines links Singapore with the world*
7 *The number of Singaporeans in tertiary institutions is on the rise*
8 *Fitness is a way of life for many*
9 *Bukit Timah Expressway*
10 *Raffles Institution*
11 *KK Women's and Children's Hospital specializes in obstetrics*
12 *A second Causeway links Singapore with Johor*
13 *The National Library*
14 *Computers are a way of life*
15 *Singapore Broadcasting Corporation. To keep up with an increasingly competitive media industry, it was revitalized as the Television Corporation of Singapore on 1 October 1994*

6

7

8

10

9

14

12

13

11

15

1

2

3

4

5

6

7

8

9

10

Wﾍile the vast majority of citizens in land-scarce Singapore live in Housing and Development Board flats, many cherish the dream of moving into private condominiums (1) or landed property (2–3) where architectural styles have become more flamboyant and exuberant. The average Singaporean cherishes traditional favourites such as satay (4) and fried noodles (9). Hawker centres (8) and their upmarket cousin, the air-conditioned food court (7), remain firmly entrenched.

1 Singapore's first suspension footbridge, completed in July 1998, enables Tanjong Rhu residents to cross the Geylang River.
2–3 Suburban architecture
4 The satay man
5 Indian sweets and savouries
6 Selling durians
7 New style food court
8 Old style hawker centre
9 Frying noodles
10 Making teh tarik

1

2

3

4

5

6

7

8

9

10

11

12

13

The 1990s have seen the performing arts go from strength to strength. The Singapore Symphony Orchestra celebrated its 20th anniversary in 1999 under Music Director Lan Shui (9). Singapore Dance Theatre (2) celebrated its 10th anniversary in 1998 under Artistic Director Goh Soo Khim. Among the enduring theatre groups are Theatreworks, whose ravishing performance of Ong Keng Sen's *King Lear* (10) received critical acclaim in Japan and Europe; and Action Theatre whose made-in-Singapore musical *Chang and Eng* (1) is based on the real life story of Siamese twins. Singapore Repertory Theatre opened the first permanent dinner theatre featuring the interactive comedy *Ah Kong's Birthday Party* (7) in 1999.

The setting up of a Film Commission will give the film industry a major boost. Among the pioneering efforts are *12 Storeys* (3), Jack Neo's *That One Not Enough* (4) and *Army Daze* (5). In television, locally produced English and Mandarin comedy and drama series have won a loyal following. English sitcoms *Phua Chu Kang* (6) and *Under One Roof* touch a unique, and not uncontroversial, chord because of their use of 'Singlish'.

The National Arts Council, established in 1991, has played a key role in nurturing the arts, spearheading the arts housing programme, which aims to provide groups with a permanent roof over their heads, and organizing the annual arts festival. In 2002, Singapore's own eagerly awaited international performing arts centre, Esplanade—Theatres on the Bay, will be ready.

---

1 *Action Theatre's 1999 musical* Chang and Eng, *based on the true life story of Siamese twins*

2 *Singapore Dance Theatre's 1994 performance of Goh Choo San's* Birds of Paradise

3 *12 Storeys, film maker Eric Khoo's 'unadorned slices of life that challenge the myth of a people thriving on Asian Values'*

4 *Jack Neo and some of the cast of his 1999 Mandarin comedy* That One Not Enough

5 *A made-in-Singapore movie:* Army Daze, *the 1996 film based on humourist Michael Chiang's play*

6 *The cast of the hit television comedy* Phua Chu Kang

7 *Eat, drink and laugh, dinner theatre with Singapore Repertory Theatre's* Ah Kong's Birthday Party

8 *Singapore Repertory Theatre's 1999 production of* M. Butterfly

9 *Music Director Lan Shui leads the Singapore Symphony Orchestra*

10 *Theatreworks' multilingual, multicultural version of* King Lear

11 *Calligrapher Pan Shou, recipient of the Meritorious Service Medal in 1994. Other recipients have included artists Chen Wen Hsi in 1992, Liu Kang in 1996 and Brother Joseph McNally in 1997.*

12 *Most of choreographer Goh Choo San's (1948–87) works were created during his 10-year association with the Washington Ballet*

13 *Kuo Pao Kun, founder of Practice Performing Arts, has nurtured Mandarin drama*

The Malay community, which constituted 14.1 per cent of the population in 1990, has made substantial advances in education and home ownership in the 1980s and 1990s. Important community organizations include the Majlis Ugama Islam Singapore (MUIS) and the Islamic Religious Council of Singapore where records are computerized (11). Mendaki is a community outreach organization set up in 1992, which uplifts educational levels and strengthens family and social values consistent with Islamic teaching.

Religious traditions and family and community ties remain strong, as these photographs illustrate. On important Islamic dates, mosques brim over with worshippers (2 and 3). Artist Iskander Jalil (1) is famed for his beautiful ceramics. Dr Yaacob Ibrahim (12) is a civil engineering lecturer and a Member of Parliament.

One price of Singapore's progress is the disappearance of the island's kampongs. Kampong Wak Selat, on the northern coast, was cleared in 1993. As writer Zuraidah Ibrahim so poignantly expressed it, '… at the core of kampong life was a spirit of neighbourliness that hung like a lovely curtain.'

2

1

3

4

5

6

7

8

9

10

11

12

*S*ingapore's Indian community is diverse and complex. 'Despite being a minority in the cosmopolitan map of Singapore—a mere 7 per cent of the total population—Indians have figured prominently in almost every field, be it politics or pedagogy, culture or commerce, scientific research of social work, law or, simply, the labour force,' writes Radhika Srinivasan in *Arpanam: A Dedication, Facets of Singapore Indians*. The nation's second elected President, S. R. Nathan (2), is a retired civil servant and former ambassador. He was sworn in on 1 September 1999.

Tamils, whose language has official status, are the longest standing and best represented of the Indian communities. Among the other smaller Indian groups, however, there has been a linguistic and cultural resurgence which has given rise to the promotion of Indian languages such as Hindi, Punjabi and Malayalam.

The formation of the Singapore Indian Development Association (SINDA) in 1991 has generated a new level of communal solidarity. The organization has made significant attempts to uplift the educational achievements of Indian students. The historic Sir Mariamman Temple (3) is a gazetted national monument. Little India, with its restaurants (16), sari boutiques and spice shops (15), remains a community hub.

9

10

11

12

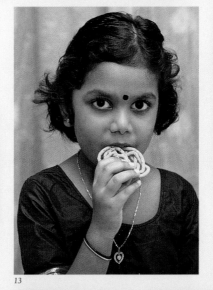

13

14

15

16

1

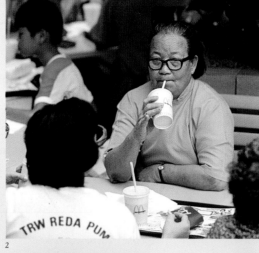

2

3

4

5

6

7

8

9

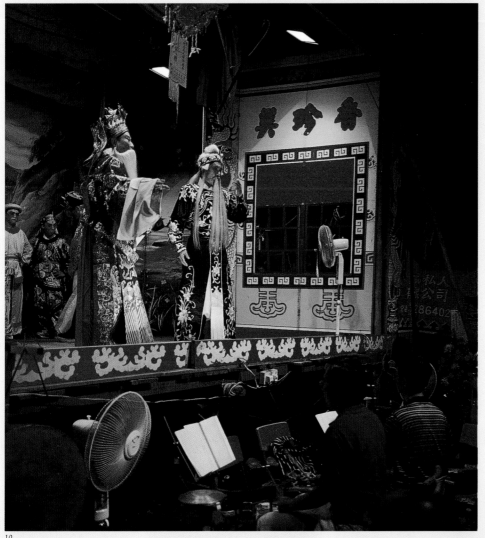

10

11

18

12

One of the most signifi-cant changes amongst the Chinese has been an increase in the use of English and Mandarin at home and a significant drop in the use of Chinese dialects. Factors which have shaped this change include the bilingual system of education and the annual Speak Mandarin Campaign, launched in 1979.

Chinese education was also given a boost with the formation of the Special Assistance Plan Schools, implemented in 1978 in response to the steadily dropping enrolment in Chinese schools. Faced with the prospect of Chinese schools dying out, the Ministry of Education reorganized the best known Chinese secondary schools as bilingual schools offering English and Chinese as first languages, thereby attracting top students from both language streams while maintaining their traditional Chinese school environment.

The traditional—Chinese opera (10), medicine halls (6 and 16), festivals (4), religious practices (17) and marriage customs (15)—and modern coexist, occasionally creating new versions of old ways. Popular Television Corporation of Singapore actress Zoe Tay (7) is the face of her generation, while Peranakan Peter Wee (9) has made heritage his business.

13

14

15

16

17

1

2

3

4

5

6

7

8

9

10

11

12

13

14

21

15

16

17

18

19

20

Getting 2 million people to think of themselves as 'Singaporean' was predicated as impossible by the sceptics who followed Singapore's first faltering steps towards nationhood. There was, however, a powerful vision. Speaking on 12 September 1965, Prime Minister Lee Kuan Yew described with passion the kind of country that would be built: 'But I say to you: here we make the model multiracial society. This is not a country that belongs to any single community: it belongs to all of us. You helped build it; your fathers, your grandfathers helped build this. There was no naval base here, and it was your labour, your father's labour which built that. My great-grandfather came here and built. Yes, he came here looking for his fortune, but he stayed—my grandfather was born here. Over a hundred years ago this was a mud-flat swamp. Today this is a modern city. Ten years from now, this will be a metropolis.'

Today, as before, Singapore's most precious resource is its people. The younger generation have experienced none of the economic instability of their parents, and the ties that bind—education and shared values—are stronger and more enduring.

Singapore the global city remains respectful of its heritage, a stance that is reflected in the view (following pages) of Chinatown restored and the financial district beyond.

SELECTED BIBLIOGRAPHY

BOOKS AND ARTICLES

Alfred, Eric (1987), *Singapore Port History 1819–1963*, Singapore: Port of Singapore Authority.

Archer, Mildred and Bastin, John (1978), *The Raffles Drawings in the India Office Library London*, Kuala Lumpur: Oxford University Press.

Bastin, John (1994), *Travellers' Singapore: An Anthology*, Kuala Lumpur: Oxford University Press.

Braga-Blake, Myrna et al. (1992), *Singapore Eurasians: Memories and Hopes*, Singapore: The Eurasian Association and Times Editions.

Brassey, Annie (1871), *The Voyage of the* Sunbeam: *Around the World in the Yacht* Sunbeam, New York: A. L. Burt.

Buckley, C. B. (1902), *An Anecdotal History of Old Times in Singapore, 1819–1867*, Singapore: Fraser & Neave; reprinted Singapore: Oxford University Press, 1984.

Cameron, John (1965), *Our Tropical Possessions in Malayan India*, Kuala Lumpur: Oxford University Press.

Chua Beng Huat (1989), *The Golden Shoe: Building Singapore's Financial District*, Singapore: Urban Redevelopment Authority.

Crawfurd, John (1828), *Journal of an Embassy from the Governor General of India to the Courts of Siam and Cochin China*, London: Henry Colburn.

Edwards, Norman (1990), *The Singapore House and Residential Life 1819–1939*, Singapore: Oxford University Press.

Edwards, Norman and Keys, Peter (1988), *Singapore: A Guide to Buildings, Streets, Places*, Singapore: Times Books International.

Falconer, John (1987), *A Vision of the Past: A History of Photography in Singapore and Malaya, The Photographs of G.R. Lambert & Co., 1880–1910*, Singapore: Times Editions.

Foran, Robert (1935), *Malayan Symphony*, London: Hutchinson.

Ford, Colin and Steinorth, Karl (1988), *You Press the Button We do the Rest: The Birth of Snapshot Photography*, London: Dirk Nishen Publishing and National Museum of Photography, Film and Television.

Hall-Jones, John (1983), *The Thomson Paintings: Mid-Nineteenth Century Paintings of the Straits Settlements and Malaya*, Singapore: Oxford University Press.

Hall-Jones, John and Hooi, Christopher (1979), *An Early Surveyor in Singapore: John Turnbull Thomson in Singapore 1841–1853*, Singapore: National Museum.

Han Fook Kwang; Fernandez, Warren and Tan, Sumiko (1998), *Lee Kuan Yew: The Man and His Ideas*, Singapore: Singapore Press Holdings and Times Editions.

Han Su Yin and Robinson, Peter (undated, c. 1954), *See Singapore*, Singapore: Donald Moore Books.

Hancock, T. H. H. (1986), *Coleman's Singapore*, Kuala Lumpur: Malaysian Branch of the Royal Asiatic Society and Pelanduk Publications.

Hon, Joan (1988), *100 Years of the Singapore Fire Service*, Singapore: Singapore Fire Service and Times Books International.

_____ (1990), *Tidal Fortunes: A Story of Change: The Singapore River and Kallang Basin*, Singapore: Landmark Books.

Iskander Mydin (1989), *Pioneers of the Streets*, Singapore: Art, Antiques and Antiquities.

Jackson, Joseph Stanley (1920), *Handbook for Travellers to Singapore*, Singapore: Far Eastern Tourist Agency.

Kaye, Barrington (1960), *Upper Nankin Street Singapore: A Sociological Study of Chinese Households Living in a Densely Populated Area*, Singapore: University of Malaya Press.

Kwa Chong Guan et al. (1989), *Tanjong Pagar, Singapore's Cradle of Development*, Singapore: Tanjong Pagar Citizens' Consultative Committee and Landmark Books.

Kwok Kian Chow (1996), *Channels & Confluences: A History of Singapore Art*, Singapore: Singapore Art Museum and Landmark Books.

Lee, Edwin (1991), *The British As Rulers: Governing Multi-racial Singapore 1867–1914*, Singapore: Singapore University Press.

Lee Kip Lin (1983), *Telok Ayer Market*, Singapore: Archives and Oral History Department.

_____ (1984), *Emerald Hill, The Story of a Street in Words and Pictures*, Singapore: National Museum of Singapore.

_____ (1987), *The Singapore House 1819–1942*, Singapore: Preservation of Monuments Board and Times Editions.

Lee, Peter and Chen, Jennifer (1998), *Rumah Baba: Life in a Peranakan House*, Singapore: National Heritage Board.

Lee Sing Kong and Chua Sian Eng (1992), *More Than a Garden City*, Singapore: Parks and Recreation Department, Ministry of National Development.

Lim Kay Tong (1991), *Cathay: 55 Years of Cinema*, Singapore: Landmark Books for Cathay Organization.

Liu, Gretchen (1991), *Raffles Hotel*, Singapore: Raffles Hotel and Landmark Books.

_____ (1995), *From the Family Album, Portraits from the Lee Brothers Studio, Singapore 1910–1925*, Singapore: National Heritage Board and Landmark Books.

_____ (1996), *In Granite and Chunam: The National Monuments of Singapore*, Singapore: Preservation of Monuments Board and Landmark Books.

Lloyd, Ian and Hoe, Irene (1985), *Singapore From the Air*, Singapore: Times Editions.

Newhall, Beaumont (1982), *The History of Photography*, New York: Museum of Modern Art and Boston: Little Brown and Company.

Saw Swee Hock (1970), *Singapore Population in Transition*, Philadelphia: University of Pennsylvania Press.

Sharp, Ilsa (1985), *The Singapore Cricket Club, 1852–1985*, Singapore: The Singapore Cricket Club.

Siddique, Sharon and Shotam-Gore, Nirmala (eds.) (1983), *Serangoon Road: A Pictorial History*, Singapore: Educational Publications Bureau.

Song Ong Siang (1922), *One Hundred Years' History of the Chinese in Singapore*, London: John Murray, reprinted by Singapore: Oxford University Press, 1984.

Su, Elizabeth (1985), 'Profile of a River', *Plannews*, Journal of the Singapore Institute of Planning, July, 10 (1).

Tay, Simon (1993), *Over Singapore*, Singapore: Archipelago Press.

Teo, Marriane; Chong Yu-Chee and Oh, Julia, *Nineteenth Century Prints of Singapore*, Singapore: The National Museum.

Thomson, John (1875), *The Straits of Malcca, Indo-China and China or Ten Years' Travel, Adventures and Residence Abroad*, London: S. Low Marston, Low & Searle; reprinted Singapore: Oxford University Press, 1992.

Thomson, John Turnbull (1864), *Glimpses into Life in Malayan Lands*, London: Richardson; reprinted Singapore: Oxford University Press, 1984.

Tinsley, Bonnie (1989), *Visions of Delight: The Singapore Botanic Gardens Through the Ages*, Singapore: Singapore Botanic Gardens.

Turnbull, C. M. (1972), *The Straits Settlements 1826–67: Indian Presidency to Crown Colony*, London: The Athlone Press of the University of London.

_____ (1977), *A History of Singapore 1819–1975*, Kuala Lumpur: Oxford University Press.

Wallace, Sir Donald Mackenzie (1912), *The Web of Empire: A Diary of the Imperial Tour of their Royal Highnesses the Duke and Duchess of Cornwall & York in 1901*, London: Macmillan and Company.

Warren, James Francis (1986), *Rickshaw Coolie: A People's History of Singapore 1880–1940*, Singapore: Oxford University Press.

Wong, Aline and Yeh, Stephen (1985), *Housing a Nation: 25 Years of Public Housing in Singapore*, Singapore: Housing and Development Board and Maruzen Asia.

Wright, Arnold and Cartwright, H. A. (eds.) (1908), *Twentieth Century Impressions of British Malaya*, London: Lloyds Greater Britain Publishing Co. Ltd.

Wright, Arnold and Reid, Thomas H. (1912), *The Malay Peninsula: A Record of British Progress in the Middle East*, London: T. Fisher Unwin.

Yen, Ching-Hwang (1986), *A Social History of the Chinese in Singapore and Malaya 1800–1911*, Singapore: Oxford University Press.

Yeoh, Brenda S. A. (1996), *Contesting Space: Power Relations and the Urban Built Environment in Colonial Singapore*, Kuala Lumpur: Oxford University Press.

York, F. W., and Phillips, A. R. (1996), *Singapore: A History of Trams, Trolley-buses and Buses, 1880s to 1960s*, Vol. 1, Croydon, United Kingdom: DTS Publishing.

Zuraidah Ibrahim (1994), *Muslims in Singapore: A Shared Vision*, Singapore: Majlis Ugama Islam Singapura and Times Editions.

CATALOGUES AND COMMEMORATIVE PUBLICATIONS

Alumni Affairs and Development Office, National University of Singapore (1993), *Raffles College, 1928–1949*, Singapore.

Archives and Oral History Department (1983), *Chinatown: An Album of a Singapore Community*, Singapore: Times Books International.

Department of Civil Aviation and Archives and Oral History Department (1982), *Singapore Fly-Past, A Pictorial Review of Civil Aviation in Singapore 1911–1981*, Singapore: MPH Magazines.

Information Division, Ministry of Culture (1984), *Singapore: An Illustrated History 1941–1984*, Singapore.

National Heritage Board (1998), *Singapore: Journey Into Nationhood*, Singapore: Landmark Books.

Organizing Committee of a Dinner by the Indian Community (1984), *Arpanam: A Dedication, Facets of Singapore Indians*, Singapore: Landmark Books.

Public Utilities Board (1985), *Yesterday and Today, The Story of Public Electricity, Water and Gas Supplies in Singapore*, Singapore: Times Books International.

Sin Chew Jit Poh and Ministry of Culture (1981), *Singapore in Pictures, 1819–1945*, Singapore.

Singapore Federation of Chinese Clan Associations, National Archives of Singapore, Oral History Department and Singapore News and Publications Ltd (1986), *History of the Chinese Clan Associations in Singapore*, Singapore.

Singapore Turf Club (1983), *Fifty Years at Bukit Timah, 1933–1983*, Singapore: Wendy Hutton Creative Services.

The Government of Singapore (1991), *Singapore: The Next Lap*, Singapore: Times Editions.

INDEX

PICTURE CREDITS